An Englishman's love affair with China's national treasure

JADE LIFE

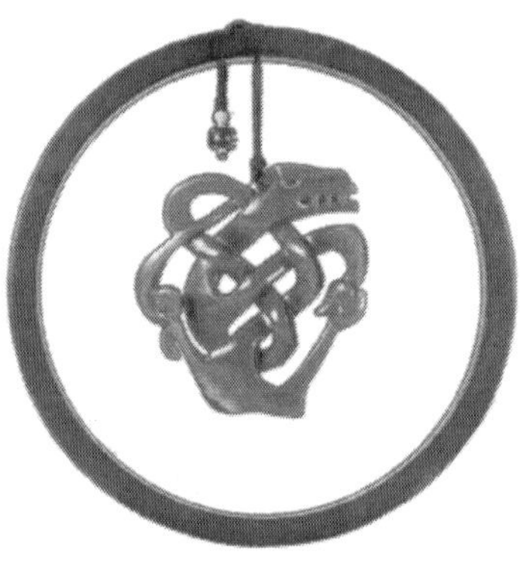

ANDREW SHAW

EARNSHAW BOOKS

Jade Life

By Andrew Shaw

ISBN-13: 978-988-8552-18-4

Cover design: Rob Osborne

ART / Asian / General

EB110

Published by Earnshaw Books Ltd. (Hong Kong)

To my Parents

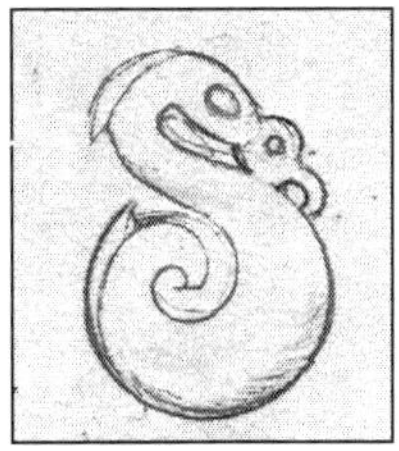

Table of Contents

NOTE: The sketches at the start of each chapter and section are preliminary designs taken from Andrew's jade carving work book.

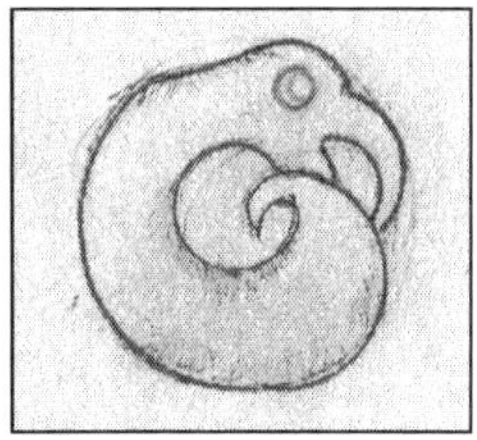

Introduction

The jade market in China is huge. Based on all I have read and heard – and there are no reliable sources for this information – I estimate it to be worth at least US$30 billion a year. You would be hard pressed to find a Chinese person who does not own some jade. Even if you did they would be still be able to tell you of some piece of jade that has been in the family for generations.

For Chinese people, jade represents everything that is pure and noble. It is mentioned in the earliest myths and legends. In the West, people talk of a stone age, but in China, ancient times included a jade age. The written character for jade is one of the oldest in the Chinese language. Confucius raved about it. Wars have been fought over it. Emperors spoke to the Gods through it. Even in the totally state-planned economy of the early decades of communist rule, factories were designated to produce and sell it.

Jade is the heart and soul of China. It is in the DNA of every citizen. And it is more popular now than it has been at any time in the country's long history. As its people have become wealthier in recent times, they have not forgotten their heritage. They value jade far more highly than diamonds or gold. In less than three decades, production has developed from a handful of state-run factories with several thousand workers worth a few million dollars a year to a huge industry with an annual turnover of billions employing nearly a million people.

I knew none of this when I first stumbled across jade many years go. I was in Thailand on a sabbatical from my job as a BBC reporter. A job I had once loved but which had come to bore me to tears.

There is a small jade industry which thrives in northern Thailand near the border with Myanmar (Burma). Jade and opium are smuggled over the border in exchange for guns and money. While most of the jade ends up in the workshops of China some of it is fashioned by Thai craftsman in and around small cities like Chiang Mai. It was at one of these workshops that I bought my first jade.

I have no idea why I walked into that workshop but I am very glad I did. I browsed for a while admiring the workmanship and then asked the very pretty salesgirl to show me a little lavender jade Buddha that for some reason had caught my eye.

With a dazzling smile and great care, she unlocked the glass case it was displayed in and placed it on a silk cloth in front of me. When I picked it up time seemed to stop. It sang to me. It calmed me. It made me smile just to look at it. I turned it round and round in my hands watching the light reflect off its polished surfaces. It sang to my soul. Cool and silky to the touch, it had an inner glow and a timelessness to it that fascinated me. I had to have it. Now many years later it sits on my desk. I still get a feeling of peace just seeing it next to me.

Buying it was one of the last things I did before returning to my life in London, but it was the first step in what was to become an all consuming passion. I started searching for all the information I could find about jade. Where did it come from? Who carved it? What were the meanings behind each carving? How much did it cost? What colors did it come in?

I wanted to know about the fresh, glowing, beautiful stones being carved in the modern world. I bought every book I could lay my hands on but most of them spoke of the past. None of them seemed to know about the stone of today. I decided that the only way I was going to do this was as to travel to the spiritual home of jade, China, and learn how to carve it myself.

I left the BBC to pursue my dream. I have never missed that great organization. I am very sure it has never missed me. If I had known how difficult my journey was going to be I may never have taken that first step but I am glad I did. I am now a gold medal winning jade carver and the only foreigner to be taught the secrets of the Chinese masters. As I sit drinking my morning coffee on the balcony of my tea house and jade gallery overlooking Jinji Lake I am content.

I have discovered a whole new world the West hardly knows exists. If you want to understand China and how its people have managed to transform their country into the economic powerhouse and world superpower it is today you need to look no further than the modern jade industry. And appreciating why this stone means so much to them, may provide an insight into the personality and determination of a country and a people who may well dominate the twenty-first century.

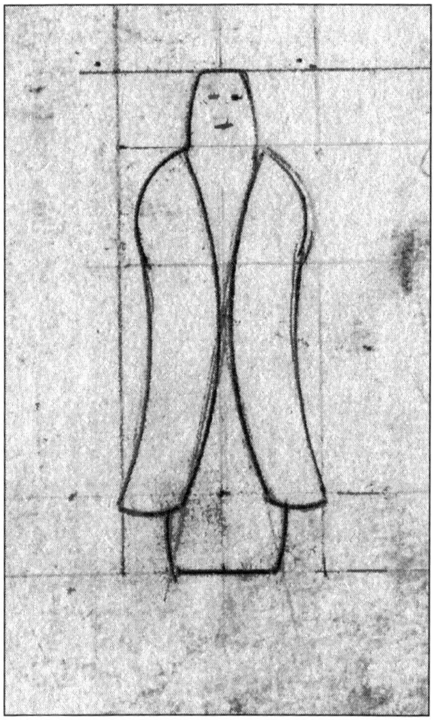

1

How Big is the Chinese Jade Industry?

I HAD ABSOLUTELY no idea how much people in China loved jade until I moved here. It is everywhere. Jade is huge in China. It's difficult to make people understand how a stone can capture the imagination of an entire nation. People spend billions of dollars a year on it. There are tens of thousands of shops selling it. Entire cities, towns and villages all over China exist just to produce jade goods for a seemingly insatiable market. Forget about the ancient jades collecting dust in museums, the modern industry has carved more jade in the twenty-first century than was previously carved in the whole of history. The quality of the jade used and the skill levels of contemporary carvers far outshine that of all previous eras.

There are workshops, large and small, churning out tens of thousands of rings, bracelets, necklaces, bangles, teapots, vases, goblets, cigarette holders, ink stands, figurines and a myriad other things in jade. Boulders weighing more than a ton are carved into works of art. Statues of Confucius, Buddha and Guanyin are made for temples, sculptures of real and mythical animals are placed in the lobbies of hotels and at the doors of major banks and corporations, even tables and chairs are made from jade. But in spite of its size it is still a cottage industry. Nearly all enterprises are family-run businesses with just a few workers or even a solitary craftsman. It is rare to find a workshop or factory with more than a few dozen people. The town of Sihui in Guangdong province has an estimated one hundred and fifty thousand people working with jade, but the largest jade factory has only fifty carvers.

These family businesses are reluctant to tell you how much money they make. Factory owners, master carvers, ordinary craftsmen and the owners of jade shops tend to be very tight lipped about how much they sell. No-one boasts about good sales. If your landlord sees you are doing well he will put your rent up, if a local official sees you making money by hook or by crook he will want his cut and tax inspectors are the same everywhere.

Thousands of tons are carved every year and millions of pieces sold to the general public. There are 1.5 billion people in China and a huge number of them will own a piece of jade. Board the subway in one of the major cities and spend an hour counting the number of people who you can see wearing jade. It could be a bangle, ring, necklace or pendant. It might just be a small piece dangling from their mobile phone. I have a keen eye for jade because I love it so much and generally speaking one in twenty people I see will be wearing it.

If you did a quick survey of everyone in your carriage you would probably find that many of them would be able to tell you the meaning behind the piece they were wearing. You will see children wearing jade. These are not trinkets but amulets of protection given to them by family members. They take their jade very seriously in China. It's in the blood, which might go a long way to explaining why the market is so big.

I knew none of this when I arrived in China. My plane landed in Shanghai and I immediately made a beeline for Suzhou. I had heard it was a place where jade was carved and travel agents called it "The Venice of the East" because it had more canals than the whole of Western Europe. It was renowned for its lazy, winding, tree lined streets and was for centuries considered to be one of the most beautiful cities in China.

I had a vision of sitting at the feet of a master beside a gently tinkling fountain in his walled garden while we discussed the finer points of carving. He would guide me through the intricacies of the ancient craft and praise me for my skill while we sipped green tea from porcelain cups. I think I may have imagined him with a Fu Manchu beard and flowing robes. There were definitely some ancients in broad-brimmed hats tending Azaleas and Chrysanthemums in the background.

The reality was that with my suitcase in one hand and my ignorance in the other, I got off the train in Suzhou and was immediately overwhelmed by noise and chaos. There were thousands of people who seemed to be aimlessly milling around shouting at one another. All the signs were in incomprehensible Chinese and the only English that I heard was "Taxi? Taxi?" and "Hotel, you want hotel?" Beggars pushed people aside to thrust their bowls under my nose. Men (and women) were hawking and spitting on the ground.

It was a rude awakening from my daydream. Suzhou may have been some Chinese idyll in a previous life but my cab journey from the station to the hotel made it clear this was no longer the case. Rapid industrialization meant that a city which twenty years before had two million inhabitants now had ten million. It was polluted, raucous and chaotic. The tree-lined boulevards had mostly disappeared and all but a few of the canals were now hidden by concrete.

This in itself was not a major problem. It added to the challenge and excitement of learning about a new culture and searching for that mythical master to teach me about jade. But the fact that no one seemed to speak English and I didn't have a word of Chinese was a major drawback. Just trying to buy a train ticket involved taking an interpreter along with me to the ticket office. How was I going to find someone to instruct me if I couldn't speak the language? How would we communicate? I had to learn Chinese – and quickly.

I got myself a little job at an English school, rented an apartment and started a full-time course in Chinese at Suzhou University. Once I had a little of the language under my belt, all my spare waking hours were spent in the hunt for a master. I suffered months of frustration. It was almost impossible to get across to people that I wanted to learn to carve jade.

It took four months before I had my first breakthrough. I was in a shop buying something to drink and struck up a conversation with the sales assistant. At that time, back in 2008, foreigners were still quite a novelty in Suzhou and most people were keen to talk to me once they realized I could handle basic Chinese. I mentioned my dream of learning to carve and asked the sales assistant if she knew where I could do this. Most of her answer was unintelligible, but she pointed across the street to a tiny alley and said "Follow the noise."

More in hope than expectation I entered the alley she had pointed to which was about two meters wide and it was as though all my Christmases had come at once. This tiny, unpaved lane was full of single-storey workshops with craftsmen hunched over spindles carving jade. In the first sixty meters I counted seventy workshops and more than a hundred and twenty craftsmen. And this was just the beginning of a maze of tiny lanes known as Xiang Wang Alley where thousands of people work with this precious stone. The hum of machinery was incessant and the whole area had a lived-in slightly seedy look. The buildings may once have been painted white, but most of that had long ago peeled off or faded away. Electricity was supplied by a tangled web of overhead power lines some of which were hanging so low you had to duck to avoid them. It was muddy underfoot and I had to step around large puddles from the recent rain as I walked from workshop to workshop.

I wandered around dazed with delight, poking my head into doorways, grinning like an idiot and admiring the workmanship. The craftsmen were very friendly. Most of them thought I was a tourist who was lost. Some wanted to take a picture with me, others tried to sell me jade. Here was somewhere I could find a teacher, I thought. It was a far cry from the ancient master in his walled garden that I had hoped for. There would be no sipping tea, or Cha, from porcelain cups in this neck of the woods, but surely there would be someone willing to help me unlock the secrets of Chinese jade carving and set me on the path to becoming a master.

It took another five months and many false starts, but I found my teacher. Chinese people often have difficulty giving a yes or no answer, so while many of them seemed to consider my request and were willing to spend hours chatting and sipping tea with me they were in fact just far too polite to say no. Even today, after years of being married to a Chinese woman, I am pretty sure the only day I have had a categorical yes or no answer from her was the day I proposed to her.

After months of knocking on doors, I met Wufan and my life changed forever. A short stocky man with an open face and a ready smile, he welcomed me into his workshop and his home. He then spent two years teaching me the basics of jade carving. He lent me the tools I needed, gave me jade to carve and shared his knowledge with little thought of return. His generosity allowed me to become the jade artist that I am today. I am forever grateful to a humble craftsman who epitomizes all that is good about China.

I was very lucky. By chance I had found a jade carving hub with a skill level unmatched anywhere else. This maze of tiny, grubby alleys tucked away in the south eastern part of the old city is in an area only eight hundred meters long and about one hundred meters at its widest, but it supplied jade shops all over the country with high quality carvings.

Crammed into this small district are about 1,500 workshops and at least four thousand people who make their living from jade. The smallest workshops are less than two meters square and only have room for one craftsman, a stool for him to sit on, his spindle and a tiny table to display jades for sale. The largest workshops are no more than twenty meters square and have four or five craftsmen working in a back room while an assistant sits with the jades for sale in display cabinets out front.

It's a bustling, thriving community where deals are made in workshops, on the phone and on doorsteps. You can walk through an archway halfway down an alley and it will open into a small courtyard filled with even more tiny workshops where craftsmen are bent over their spindles, haggling with customers or hunched in small groups appraising jade. And if it was busy back then, it is far busier now. Jade has increased in popularity so much since I arrived here that more and more workshops have opened and spilled out into neighboring streets. The roads surrounding the alleys have filled up with hundreds more jade shops. Close by there is a huge high end jade mall with another one hundred and fifty air conditioned outlets inside. In addition to this numerous apartments in the surrounding housing compounds have been taken over and converted into workshops. Rents in the jade carving alleys are now so high that craftsmen who have worked there for years have moved out seeking cheaper workspaces. A new workshop has opened every week in and around this jade carving area alone since I first discovered it.

I spent some very happy years here learning the basics of my craft. I opened my first workshop here. I look back on it as one of the happiest times of my life.

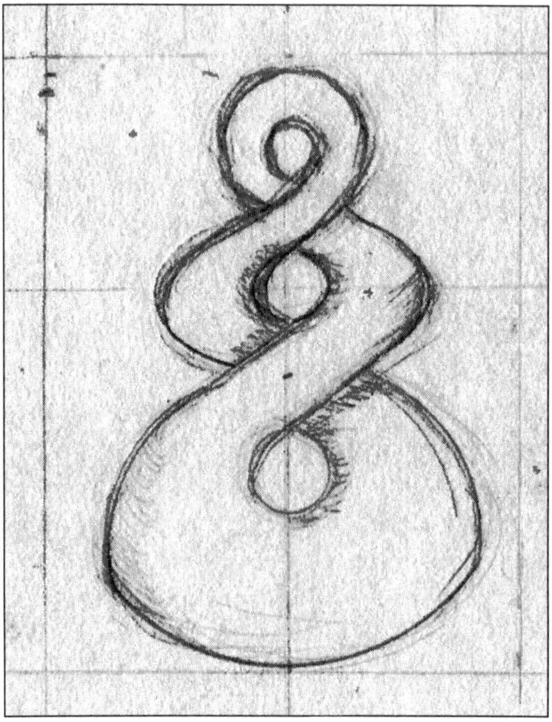

2

Why do Chinese people love Jade?

Jade is embedded in the Chinese psyche. It's been part of Chinese culture for so long it's almost as though it's in the DNA. The earliest Chinese myths talk of jade. The Goddess Nüwa, to save the world from destruction, repaired a rent in heaven by grinding five different colored stones together. What was left of the stones fell to Earth as dust and turned to jade.

Jade was ideal to use as a tool because it is so tough. You can make an axe out of jade and chop down a tree with it. It was used for adornment because of its beauty. Emperors used jade as a medium to speak to heaven. For thousands of years it was used in religious rituals.

Ancient royalty knew its value. Nearly four thousand years ago they stole it for themselves. The symbol or character for king in the Shang Dynasty is a representation of three jade discs strung on a cords and the Chinese characters for "king" and "jade" are almost identical, different by only one little stroke.

Chinese people have associated jade with immortality and long life for millennia. Drinking powdered jade was for long ages thought to prolong life, although it probably shortened it. Most people have heard of the famous jade suits that royalty were once buried in more than two thousand years ago. It was believed the jade would preserve the body. It didn't of course. More than twenty such burial suits have now been discovered but in each case they were wrapped around crumbled skeletons.

At one time people were buried with a jade cicada in their mouths, the cicada representing rebirth. This is because ancient Chinese people believed cicadas returned from the dead, a belief that came about because the cicada spends its pre-adult life deep underground and only emerges from the earth - as if from the grave - fully formed.

Jade has been associated in some way with nearly every religion. Taoism names the head of the pantheon of Chinese gods as the Jade Emperor, who lives in a jade palace, on a jade mountain, at the foot of which is the jade lake on the shores of which is the jade tree which bears the fruit of immortal life. This home of the gods is supposed to be in the Kunlun Mountains, which roughly forms the northern edge of the Tibetan plateau, where the best jade comes from.

Buddhism adopted jade very early on. There are temples which are famous for their jade Buddhas. The Laughing Buddha is a very popular carving. Tens if not hundreds of thousands of Buddha pendants are carved and sold every year. The Laughing Buddha is so common that it even has an entry in Chinese dictionaries. Guanyin, the Goddess of Mercy and Compassion, who hears all the woes of the world is just as popular a Buddhist carving. Even the early Christian missionaries to China had crucifixes and rosaries made out of jade.

Jade has always been revered in China and largely due to Confucius, people associate it with all that is good and pure. Two and a half millennia ago, the great philosopher said it embodied purity, intelligence, justice, loyalty, truth, sincerity and chastity. He wrote that its iridescent brightness represented heaven and being born of mountain and of water it represented the earth. He also said the pure note which it gave forth when struck represented music.

This is so true. When I give talks on jade, I start by striking a jade gong. It usually silences a room because a polished jade gong when struck makes a sound as pure and sweet as you are likely to hear. Confucius knew this. He played the "Stones" as they were called. These were polished jades, which when struck, gave off a variety of notes. He was said to be quite an expert.

The first truly comprehensive Chinese dictionary, written in the early part of the second century A.D. by Xu Shen, defined jade as a stone of beauty. Xu Shen compared its texture, luster, color, translucence and its melodious sound when struck to the five virtues of benevolence, righteousness, propriety, wisdom and fidelity. A famous saying in China is "The virtues of a gentleman may be likened to jade."

There are hundreds of Chinese sayings which use the word

jade - almost always in a positive context - as something good, noble, beautiful or honest - reinforcing the cultural belief that jade is something associated with the best in humankind. "Words of Jade and Gold", for example, means to praise someone for their invaluable advice. "As Pure as Jade and clean as Ice" means pure and noble. The phrase "Jade lady" refers to a woman of beauty. Beautiful women are also described as smooth as jade and as soft as flowers. A woman with a fair complexion and a slim figure is described as having jade bones and ice white skin.

In the West, we might say to someone, "You should treat your body like a temple." In Chinese they say, "Cherish the body as if it was jade." Chinese people say good friends are like gold and jade. The Bible talks of beating swords into ploughshares but in the Middle Kingdom they talk of exchanging weapons for jade and silk. In English, we might warn someone that all that glitters is not gold. In Chinese they will tell you what appears to be jade and gold on the outside is rubbish on the inside.

Someone who can't tell the difference between good and bad is referred to as someone who can't tell jade from stone. When someone dies, we might say they have gone to heaven but in China they might tell you that someone is now taking orders at the jade palace. Jade Stalk is used for the male sexual organ. Jade Gate is used for the female equivalent.

Jade is also ever present in Chinese literature. One of the four great Chinese classics, the eighteenth-century novel, *Dream of the Red Chamber*, includes two main characters called Precious Jade and Black Jade. Precious Jade was born with a piece of pure jade in his mouth. This piece of bright stone, left over from Nüwa's repair of the dome of heaven, is an integral part of the novel. The Jade Emperor features prominently in *Journey to the West*, the sixteenth-century Ming Dynasty classic, better known in the West as *Monkey*.

More recently, in the last decade of the twentieth century, a novel called *The Jade King* by Huo Da, about three generations of Muslim jade carvers in Beijing, became so popular that it was made into a film. I named my first jade workshop and gallery after a character in the book, a man so obsessed with jade that when he heard about anyone who had jades, he would knock on their door and ask to see them and then spend hours poring over them, fondling the jades and admiring their beauty. He was known as the Jade Fiend.

In China, thousands of books have been published in the last few decades alone about jade. There are encyclopedias about jade, multi-volume illustrated sets of the history of jade and books about every aspect of the stone that you can think of. Most decent bookshops have a whole section devoted to jade, and if not a whole section then a large number of books in the arts and crafts section or on the shelves devoted to Chinese culture will be about it.

Folklore is full of tales about this precious stone. One story tells us that jade is the tears shed by the dragon when China was overrun by the Tartars – that is, the Mongols in the thirteenth century. There is the story of the craftsman who carved his young daughter a jade bracelet so exquisite that over the years its fame spread far and wide. The Emperor's concubine heard about it and demanded that he obtain it for her. When soldiers went to take it, they had to hack off her hand to get it and as a result of her being maimed, her husband-to-be refused to marry her. She ended up in a convent where she learned the art of swordmanship. One day, she disappeared and a few days later the Emperor and his concubine were found dead. A sword had been used to kill them. The tale does not recount what happened to the nun or the exquisite jade bracelet.

In the West, we talk of a Man in the Moon. In China they

talk of the Jade Rabbit in the Moon. He stands by the side of the Moon Goddess, Chang'e, and mixes the elixir of immortality with a pestle and mortar.

Jade has been part of the culture for so long that it is just accepted as part of life. There are those in China who worry that as the country modernizes this heritage will be forgotten. They need not be concerned. Jade is fixed too deeply in the Chinese psyche. For example, when China was planning to land its first unmanned probe on the moon, there was a poll to see what it should be called. The overwhelming vote was to call it the Jade Rabbit. Chinese people have not forgotten their heritage.

At a subconscious level, jade seems to have entered the soul of China. I think the best example of this is when the post-1949 communist government simplified the ancient Chinese language, they changed the character for "country" to a piece of jade enclosed by four protective walls: 国. For a regime that wanted a fresh start and to stamp out all things traditional, it seems strange that they would choose to include the symbol for jade in the new character for the communist state. I can only assume jade had become so much part of Chinese culture that even hardened communists didn't think it was odd or inappropriate.

Today jade is accepted as one of the most important parts of Chinese culture. Its full rehabilitation was demonstrated during the 2008 Olympics in which the main material used for the making of the gold, silver and bronze medals was jade. Sales of jade rocketed after that. A sure sign, perhaps, that jade was seen as a symbol not only of the ancient middle kingdom but also of modern China.

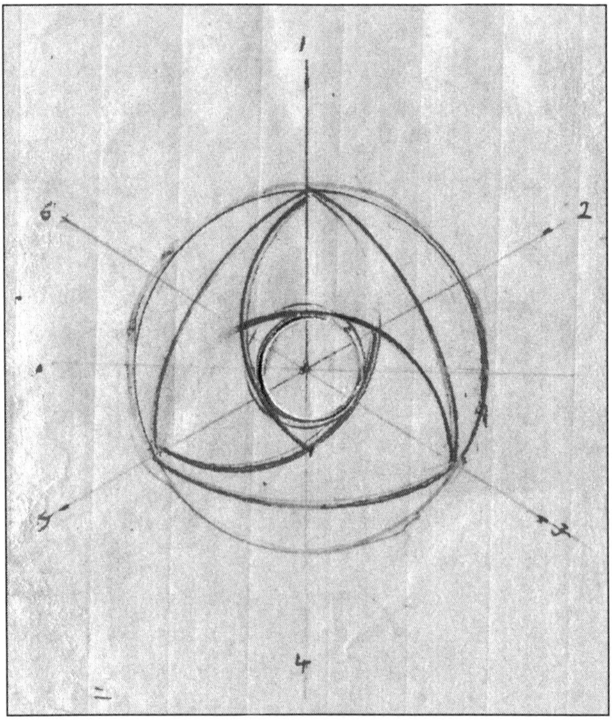

3

WHAT IS JADE?

JADE IS AN UMBRELLA term used to describe two different stones. The first is nephrite, which has been carved in China for thousands of years. The second is jadeite, which was only introduced to China from Burma in the late eighteenth century. Although similar in appearance, they are chemically and structurally different. Stone

Age cultures all over the world used these two rocks for either tools, weapons, ritual or adornment.

Nephrite use was more common. It was used by tribes on both the Pacific and Atlantic coasts of North America, stone age Europe and in Southeast and East Asia, especially in what is now China. Before the discovery of metal it was the nearest thing neolithic man had to metal tools and weapons. It's a very tough material. At the same time, it is hard but not so hard that it can't be ground to shape by harder materials like quartz. It takes time and patience, but you can grind it to a sharp edge. It is also quite a heavy material, so if you make an axe head or adz out of it you can wield it with enough force to chop down a tree or strike a killing blow.

Russell Beck, the great New Zealand carver, once tested how jade tools performed compared to metal. Among other things, he fashioned a twist drill which bored holes in wood and aluminum without effort, a cold chisel which sheared a 1mm steel plate, and even jade nails which he hammered into timber.

Nephrite comes in a variety of attractive colors and the best of it is beautifully translucent. It can be found in many shades of green but it also comes in white, black, a mixture of white and black known as porcelain, grey, brown, blue and yellow.

The finest nephrite is also soft to the touch. It's a very tactile stone which is why some Chinese people carry a pebble around with them. They call these pocket jades "worry" or "meditation" pieces.

While most Stone Age cultures abandoned nephrite once they started using metal tools, this was not the case in ancient China. It was already so much part of life they continued to use it for adornment and ritual.

Jadeite, on the other hand, is a baby in the world of Chinese jade. Legend has it that sometime in the thirteenth-century a merchant from Yunnan, traveling through what is now northern Myanmar (Burma), picked up a boulder to balance the load on his mule. When it was broken open, the brown-skinned rock revealed a vivid, "emerald" green material.

Expeditions were sent from Yunnan to find the source of this unusual material but they were unsuccessful. Although occasional small pieces of green jadeite would appear in China over the next five hundred years, their origin remained a mystery until the late eighteenth century during the reign of the Emperor Qianlong.

It has been suggested that he launched a series of invasions into Burma in an effort to annex the mines which produced this wonderful stone. Conventional histories, however, regard these campaigns as just one of the many frontier wars carried out during his reign. Whatever the truth of the matter there is no doubt the emperor adored this stone, especially the brilliant kingfisher green variety. His subjects followed his lead and it was soon rivaling nephrite as the stone of choice.

Jadeite is also a very tough stone and takes a great polish. It is brighter, harder and the colors are more vivid than those found in nephrite. This is perhaps one of the reasons that Chinese people adore it. They love bright colors. It comes in many shades of green and in various shades of purple and lavender. There is also blue, black, brown, grey and yellow jadeite. Some of the best pieces have several colors in them.

Chinese people don't use the terms jade, jadeite and nephrite. They are all relatively new words in the English language. Chinese people have their own words for the precious stones that they have been shaping for more than eight thousand years. The core word is *Yu* (pronounced Yew), a Chinese pictogram that is thousands of years old, far older than the West's interest in the Middle Kingdom and jade. There are more than a dozen other pictogram words that contain that element and describe some form or nature of jade.

The English word, jade, is a result of misunderstanding, bad translation and the sixteenth-century equivalent of urban myth. It was first used to describe a stone brought back from Central America by the Spanish conquistadores. It was believed it had magical or at least medicinal properties to cure kidney ailments. This stone became known as *Piedra de Ijada,* which translates as Stone of the Flanks. A bad translation into French turned this into *Le Jade.* The English further shortened this to Jade and later began to use the word to describe the beautiful carved stones that came out of China.

The word nephrite is also the result of a belief that jade has medicinal properties. It derives from the Greek word *nephrites* or kidneys. It is first mentioned around the end of the seventeenth century as a green stone from Spain and the Indies which could cure kidney stones.

The Western world didn't realize for quite some time that what they called jade was two different stones. In 1863 a French chemist, Alexis Damour, analyzed both stones and named the one from Burma, jadeite, to distinguish it from the nephrite carved in China.

I have no doubt that Chinese people always knew the difference between nephrite and jadeite. The Chinese call jadeite, *fei cui* which translates as "kingfisher green", as the best of it reminded them of the brilliant green plumage of the kingfisher. The nephrite from Hetian in north west China was simply called *hetian yu* which translates as Hetian Jade.

In the modern Chinese jade industry jadeite is often referred to as Hard Jade or *ying yu* and nephrite as Soft Jade or *ruan yu.* While jadeite is harder than nephrite, nephrite is most definitely not soft. The Chinese call it soft jade because it is a very tactile stone and soft and soapy to the touch.

I need to stress that these are the two stones carved by the modern jade industry. None of the ancient jades of China were jadeite, as it has only been carved in China since the late eighteenth century. Only one of them was nephrite. Chinese scholars write about the four great ancient jades of China which are Hetian, Xiuyan, Dushan and Lantian jade. These are all stones which have been carved since before the time of Christ. Only Hetian jade, is nephrite. Lantian jade and Xiuyan jade are serpentines. Dushan jade, also known as Nanyang jade, is composed of three different minerals I can't even pronounce.

Archaeological digs have uncovered carved stones of more than twenty varieties in tombs and graves from all over China. Most of these have been nephrite but they also include serpentine, bowenite, carnelian and agate. Even today, agate and carnelian are popular carvings. Carnelian is often called Red Jade or *hong yu* and and agate is known as *yu sui* (pronounced Yew Sway).

But among the four great jades, nephrite seemed to have a special place. It is the one most commonly found in tombs and most of the jades in museums in the West are nephrite. In the modern world, along with jadeite, it is accepted as one of the two true jades. When Chinese businessmen go abroad in search of raw material for the modern jade industry they are always looking for these two stones.

A lot of people in the West still believe that all jade is green. This is perhaps not surprising as the most famous jade in the world is the fabulous kingfisher green jadeite. In addition to this, reputable dictionaries such as the Oxford English Dictionary and Merriam Webster, define jade as "typically green." In New Zealand, where there is a small carving industry, they even call it "Greenstone" but most Chinese people don't think of jade as having just one color. In my city of Suzhou most of the jade for sale is white nephrite.

So to sum up. The Chinese word *yu* (玉) has been used for thousands of years to describe any beautiful or precious carved stone. As the world became smaller and Europeans began to make inroads into China they started to use their own word, jade, to describe these stones. As time went by, they decided the only true jades were nephrite and jadeite. Today, only jadeite and nephrite are accepted around the world as jade.

And a final note. The stone that Spanish traders brought back from Central America in the sixteenth-century that they believed could cure kidney ailments later turned out to be jadeite. They had no idea that it had been used for about three thousand years for ornaments, tools and in burial rites by the Olmec, Maya and Aztec civilizations in what is now Mexico, Guatemala, Honduras and El Salvador.

The Central American stone doesn't compare to the legendary kingfisher green jadeite from the Kachin Hills in Myanmar. This is now very rare. There might seem to be a lot of it for sale in the markets and bazaars of southern China but in at least 99% of cases the color is either fake or at least "enhanced." More on that later.

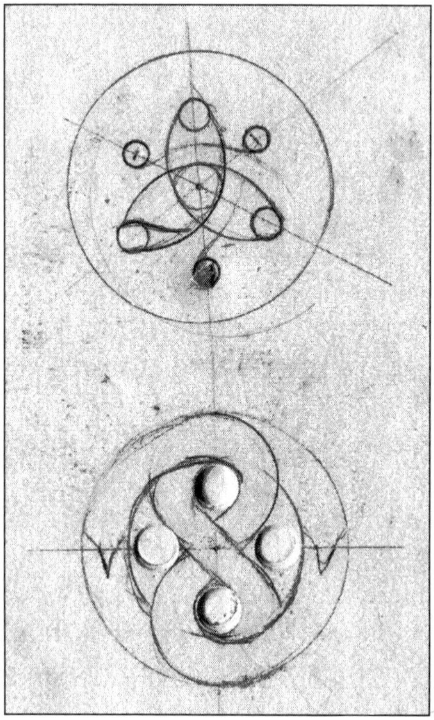

4

Where Does Jade Come From?

The modern Chinese jade industry uses thousands of tons of jade a year. About half of this is nephrite and a lot of it is mined in China. The most valuable nephrite is the mutton-fat-white jade which comes from the White Jade River, the Yurungash, that flows through Hetian just north of the Kunlun Mountains in the

Xinjiang region of northwest China. It has been treasured for thousands of years and was sent as tribute to Chinese emperors for centuries. It has become part of national folklore.

Everybody in China knows about Hetian jade. Many can recount some of the myths and folk tales that surround it. My favorite (and there are many variations of this story) is about how beautiful maidens would strip naked and step into the White Jade River by the light of a full moon to search for jade. They would easily find it as their bare feet felt among the pebbles and boulders on the river bed because their female yin would attract the male yang of the precious stone.

A more believable story is how a line of men, wearing nothing but a loincloth and a pouch, would wade through the water searching the river bed. They would be watched with eagle eyes by a clerk and a drummer seated on the bank. Each time a man stooped down to pick up a stone the drum would be struck and a mark recorded against his name. At the end of the day, the men would get out of the water and the number of marks against each name would have to tally with the number of stones in their pouch. Woe betide the man who had fewer pebbles than marks recorded.

Jade found on the river bed or buried in the river banks is called *zi liao,* or seed jade. This is jade which at some point broke off from the rock face high up in the mountains and tumbled into one of the many streams that feed the White Jade River. Over thousands of years, it rolled down to the valley below. This is the highest quality jade because by the time the stone reaches the valley floor, the softer outer material has been worn away until all that is left is the pure kernel of the stone.

Even then, only a small portion of these pebbles and boulders are the fabled mutton-fat-white jade. Hetian seed jade can also be found in many other colors including various shades of green and something called ink jade which is such a dark green that it appears to be black. One of my favorites is called porcelain jade, which seems unique to this area and consists of layers of black and white jade in the same stone.

The mutton-fat-white is now very rare. Only about fifteen to twenty kilos are found every year. The larger boulders, which might weigh between one and two kilos are the most reasonably priced at about half a million dollars. These have tiny indentations all over them like the pores of human skin. They also usually have a brown outer coloring caused by oxidization. The smaller creamy white pebbles, which also have the tell-tale tiny pores and brown skin, are much more expensive, the best can cost up to US$1,500 a gram.

Parcels of land along the river are leased to those seeking this treasure. Heavy machinery gouges ever deeper and the stones they dig up are sifted through by workers in the hope of finding mutton-fat-white. Security is very tight, and as in the past, the sifters are watched with an eagle eye and often searched at the end of each shift. Someone who manages to smuggle out one small pebble of the very finest jade, weighing twenty or thirty grams, could sell it for five years wages.

The mutton-fat-white rarely reaches the open market. It is flown straight to the workshops of master carvers who can command astronomical prices for pieces made from this material. The search for this stone is now so intense that the river bed and both banks of the river have been gouged by bulldozers and diggers from the town itself to the foot of the Kunlun Mountains about forty kilometers away. The use of this heavy machinery has turned the area into a real eyesore with both banks heaped with stones and pebbles cast aside because they were not jade. These tailings are in piles far taller than a man as far as the eye can see.

There is also the Black Jade River – the Karakash – which runs through Hetian. Seed jade is found here as well, but the stone in this sister river is rarely of the same quality. There are no bulldozers and diggers tearing up the earth. Instead, individuals dig with spades in the hope of finding this treasure. In all, about a hundred tons of seed jade are found every year in and around the two rivers but most of it is very poor quality and is sold to tourists at outrageous prices in a long winding market along the banks of the Yurungash.

Local prospectors can also take their spades and go further upstream into the foothills of the Kunlun Mountains to search for stone. They will not find seed jade. If they are lucky, they will find what is called flowing-water-jade *shan liu shui* in the mountain streams which feed the White and Black Jade rivers.

This is jade that still hasn't found its way down to the valley floor. It is not as good as the seed jade. It might have the beginnings of an oxidized skin but the small pores that cover each stone will not be as fine as those covering the jade found in the valley below.

This flowing-water-jade is still far superior to the jade which is found further up the mountainside at an altitude of between 2,000 and 2,500 meters where the air is thin. This jade has to be hacked out of the rockface itself. Craftsmen at the top end of the profession don't really consider this to be jade because it hasn't traveled to the valley floor and settled on the river bed. They call it mountain-jade and consider it a work in progress.

I have been to Hetian three times. The first time I went was as a pilgrimage to the source of the fabled mutton-fat-white jade. I was almost held hostage by my hotel because I refused to pay for a chair it was claimed I had broken. This chair was in the little jade shop in the lobby. They were all smiles until it was clear I wasn't going to buy anything, then demands were made for money because of a crack in the chair I sat on. The arrival of two police officers saved the day for me.

My second trip was to try to find a good enough piece of white jade to carve a bangle to give to my then future wife as a betrothal gift. I didn't find the stone I wanted and while I was in the jade market someone was stabbed to death in an argument over a piece of jade.

It is an uneasy place where I have never felt welcome. The last time I was there I found it difficult to leave the town because whenever I went to the bus station to buy a ticket, the sales assistant stood up and walked away – only to return to serve the next customer when I had left. I have no intention of going back.

A lot of jade is found in the Kunlun Mountains. Some is close to Hetian but most is mined six hundred kilometers to the east close to the town of Qiemo. Nearly all of it is white and pale green jade. The best of it is called *tang bai,* which translates as sugar white. This doesn't mean it's white in color like sugar, just that it is a white jade with an outer rind the color of brown sugar. Most carvers discard the brown outer skin and use the white.

I have only made one trip to Qiemo. It is no tourist destination, It is an unprepossessing place hanging on the edge of nowhere and reliant on the wholesale jade market. It's for people in the trade serious about buying in quantity. There is a fenced-off compound within the town inside of which is a large building with five deep cellars full of tons of this precious stone. I walked in with a group of serious buyers who were offered a thousand kilos of light green at about US$100 a kilo. Once it became clear they only wanted 300 kilos, they were shown the door as time wasters. After this, my intention of making an offer on five kilos died on my lips.

The biggest mining company in the area extracts about a thousand tons a year. It runs its own large wholesale market.

You need to come with a deep pocket book and a small truck if you want to do business. On my visit, there were about two hundred lots, locked in metal cages, with at least a hundred kilos of white jade in each. You have to purchase the entire contents of the cage – they won't break it up. That amounts to more than twenty tonnes of mountain jade on sale at any one time. With the wholesale price of good mountain white at about US$750 a kilo I calculated there was jade worth between fifteen and twenty million dollars in that room when I was there.

When you consider that about 1,500 tons of jade is mined in the Kunlun Mountains alone (not including Hetian), that means annual sales close to a billion dollars in uncut jade – and that is at wholesale prices before it is carved and sold at a considerable mark up.

Plus that is just at the official markets. It doesn't take into account the independent miners who climb high into the mountains and hack and blast jade out of the rock face. They make their way back to Qiemo with a load of precious stone and haggle with eager customers in the bars and tea houses over the price.

There are also a few jade shops in the town but the quality of what they had on sale was questionable at best. I did find one jade shop with some good jades at reasonable prices where they seemed honest. For those who are interested the address is 新疆且末县石一条街. There is no address in English. No one I met in Qiemo spoke English. That was a while ago though. Things might have changed.

Jade is also mined in Qinghai province to the south of the Kunlun Mountains. This can be a beautiful clear white but it doesn't have the creamy translucent opaqueness found in Hetian jade which is so admired. It fetches very good prices but the quality of it is nowhere near as good. You can easily differentiate between the two. Qinghai jade seems more crystalline and doesn't have the same soft, soapy, tactile feel of good Hetian stone. It also seems to be a harsher, brighter white. I don't know exactly how much of this is mined each year, but I see a lot more of it in the markets and shops than the sugar white jade from Qiemo. I do know that about two thousand tons of green jade is mined in Qinghai. Among this is the super hard, dense, dark green jade which is ideal for making paper-thin, delicate vases, cups and teapots that are valued so highly. A tea set made from the very best of this jade by an acknowledged master carver will set you back at least US$100,000.

Miners also unearth about twenty tons of yellow jade in Qinghai province per year, but this is harder and harder to come by. They dig deeper and deeper and find less and less.

Nephrite is also mined commercially in Liaoning province northeast of Beijing. About thirty tons are found there annually.

Although thousands of tons a year is found in China, this is not enough to satisfy the market. Chinese merchants scour the world for nephrite. Five hundred tons of green jade is imported every year from British Columbia in Canada. Two hundred tons of white and twenty tons of green comes from around Lake Baikal in Siberia in Russia. There are thirty-seven large deposits that have been identified in that area. Four of them are commercially mined and produce fine white and green jade.

The best Russian white is second only to mutton-fat-white in quality. The river-worn boulders that come from Siberia are very similar to Hetian seed jade. They are similar enough for some unscrupulous traders to try to sell them as the fabled Hetian stone.

Siberian green jade is probably the best in the world that is commercially available. New Zealand jade rivals it but the Maori won't sell it. Chinese merchants look with covetous eyes at the fine green jade on South Island in New Zealand. The Maori are not playing ball. They appreciate it's not only their heritage but a dwindling natural resource. By law, only descendants of the Maori tribe that used to rule the area where the best jade is found can take it from the land. Even then, they are limited to taking what they can carry away by themselves. This has led some New Zealand carvers with European roots who are desperate for good material to search their family trees in the hope of finding a Maori ancestor. For some reason this law does not include jade pebbles found on beaches. These are fair game for anyone.

There was once some very fine emerald green and apple green nephrite found in Wyoming in the United States but Wyoming has been picked almost clean. There are still some fabulous pieces, but most of them are in private collections. When they come up for auction they are bought for very high prices.

Tons more white and very pale green comes from a mine in Chuncheon in South Korea. As well as being a working mine, producing tons of jade each year, it is also offers tours. It's very popular. You can even get a steam bath or sauna there and of course there is a retail opportunity to buy some jade on your way out. The publicity brochures claim it is the only white jade mine in the world. A few miners in Russia and China might disagree. It might not be able to make the claim that it is a white jade mine much longer. The good white from Korea seems to be running out. I could buy it in the markets five years ago but it no longer seems available at any price.

But new sources of nephrite are being found all the time. It is now being imported from places such as Yemen and Pakistan. The world is becoming aware of the value of jade to Chinese people and a few canny miners are now turning their attention to finding new sources of a material that has a ready market. There is one company in North America which is investing millions identifying new jade deposits with a view to selling the mineral rights to Chinese buyers.

The importation of huge quantities of nephrite to China is a result of the massive expansion of the jade industry since the early 1990s, but there is also a long tradition of Chinese people sending jade back from abroad. Fireside tales which may or not be true surround this trade. The discovery of jade in Canada is attributed to Chinese workers coming across it as they worked on building a railroad through Fraser Canyon in British Columbia in the late nineteenth century. Another myth surrounding Canadian jade is that it was smuggled back to China in the coffins of workers killed while building the railroad. None of this can be proved, but experienced miners in the modern Canadian jade industry say that old nephrite pieces recorded in China long before exports officially took off look remarkably like Canadian jade.

Myths also surround the discovery and export of the fabulous emerald and apple green nephrite found in Wyoming. Again this is attributed to Chinese people working on a railroad in the 1860s and again there is little proof of this but there are records around this time of an American-Chinese businessman purchasing a large consignment and sending it to Beijing.

The late Bob Frey, one of the founding members of Friends of Jade, a defunct newsletter which originated in the U.K. in the 1980s for jade lovers, was convinced on a visit to Hong Kong in the 1990s that he saw a number of pieces which were carved from Wyoming nephrite.

I believe Chinese people have actually been buying nephrite on a regular basis from Wyoming since the mid-nineteenth century. In about 2010, I bumped into a highly respected Suzhou carver at a gem fair in Tucson. He was there to meet a man from Wyoming with a view to buying a sixty-kilo boulder of apple green jade. He did buy it, at a fraction of the price similar quality stone would cost him in China.

While there are plenty of places in China and around the world with significant deposits of nephrite that can be found, this is not the case with jadeite. There are only two places where jadeite is mined commercially: China's neighbor Myanmar, and Guatemala in Central America. At least ten thousand tons a year is currently imported from Myanmar. According to sources in the Jade Department of China's main Gem and Jewelry Association, Chinese merchants spent US$1.5 billion at the annual auction there in 2017. A lot of jadeite is also smuggled over the Myanmar-China border, which leaks like a sieve.

Modern mining techniques are used to extract the stone from what is now one of the biggest open mines in the world. Small mountains are leveled to find the pebbles and boulders which are sold at auction to gaggles of Chinese merchants.

Buying jadeite has always been a very risky process. All boulders have a very thick oxidized skin and it is impossible to tell what color jade lies beneath. Windows are cut into the stone to give bidders an idea of what is inside but it is possible for that window to show an inch of brilliant green jade only for the buyer to find that once they have cut the stone open the rest is worthless. But the rewards are so great that people are willing to take the risk. A jade bangle of the purest green jadeite can fetch more than one million U.S. dollars. A matched pair was sold at auction in Hong Kong in 2014 for nearly four million.

While jadeite is a relatively new stone to China in Central America it dates back thousands of years to the Olmecs who flourished there from about 1500 BC to 400 BC. The later Mayan and Aztec civilizations also revered it. There was a belief that the stone had powers to heal the sick and even bestow immortality. It had great symbolic and ritual value and was used for ornaments, tools and burial artifacts.

When the Conquistadores captured the Aztec emperor, Montezuma, he is said to have been surprised that they wanted gold rather than jade as a ransom. One story relates that although the Aztec ruler was virtually a prisoner, the leader of the conquistadors, Hernan Cortez, treated him as an honored guest. Each day they would meet and play a board game which was the local equivalent of chess. They would often exchange gifts. One day Montezuma presented Cortez with some fine gold and silver discs. Noting his pleasure, the next day he presented the conquistador with three beads of flawless jade. Seeing the disappointment in the face of Cortez he explained that they were his most precious possession and each bead was worth two loads of gold. Cortez was not convinced. He demanded gold.

The Aztecs faded into history. Their cities disappeared into the jungle. The art of jade carving and the source of jadeite were lost to memory. It wasn't until the 1970s that it was discovered again in what is now Guatemala by two Americans, Jay and Mary Lou Ridinger.

Ironically, while Cortez and his conquistadores did not recognize the true value of this jadeite, Chinese merchants did. Following the rediscovery of the source, it wasn't long before they came calling. Now, instead of conquistadores stealing all the gold, it is Chinese merchants smuggling all the jade. Hundreds of tons are exported illegally with government officials and customs officers bribed to ease its way out of the country and into the workshops of China.

While there are no exact figures for the amount of nephrite and jadeite used in the Chinese jade industry, it is probably fair to say that at least twenty thousand tons is carved every year. The amount is unlikely to decrease. As China becomes wealthier more and more people seem to want to buy it, the problem may be finding sufficient supplies of high-quality stone to satisfy the market.

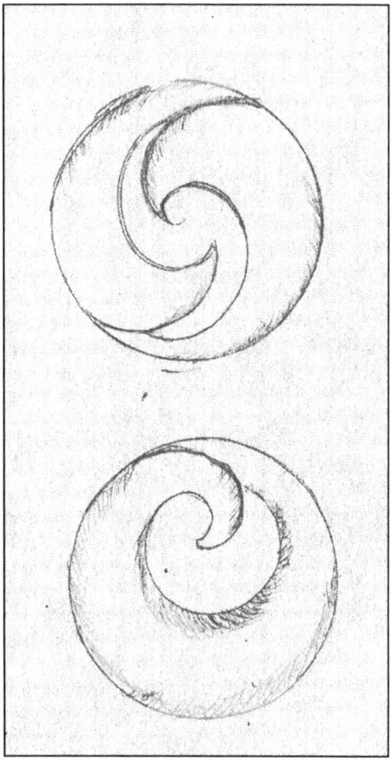

5

Jadeite Carving Centers

In 1937, Japan went to war with China. It was the beginning of a very dark period in the history of Chinese jade carving. Millions died in the war from violence and famine and few people had the money or inclination to buy jade, so very little was carved. Things got no better after the Japanese were defeated. There was soon a full-scale civil war between the communists and nationalists and by the time Mao Zedong took control of mainland China in 1949, jade carving had virtually disappeared.

But it didn't die out. Jade was too much part of Chinese culture and while there were very few customers and workshops all over China closed, some craftsmen continued the tradition.

Ironically, it was the communists who began a jade revival in the late 1950s. They may have frowned on all things traditional that reminded them of the dynasties of the past but China was dirt-poor and needed valuable foreign currency. The Middle Kingdom was still famous for its jade and there was demand from abroad. So factories were set up in Beijing, Shanghai, Guangzhou, Suzhou, Yangzhou and several other cities. Old craftsmen were recruited to man the workshops and train new carvers.

Business slowly grew and by the 1970s the factories were doing a very brisk trade. At their height the larger ones like Beijing employed a thousand people. The smaller ones like Suzhou had three hundred workers. They produced copies from previous dynasties but the work was often of a very high standard. Businessmen from Taiwan, Hong Kong, Europe and North America came calling.

When China began to open up to the West in the 1980s, sales were boosted as the businessmen and jade traders were joined by growing numbers of tourists who visited these factories to buy jade. By the end of the decade, jade carvers began to realize they no longer needed to work for a pittance in a state factory and they started to open their own workshops. Many of those in the Guangzhou factory headed home to the small sleepy town of Sihui about fifty kilometers to the west. They had been recruited from there in the first place because of its tradition of jadeite carving. Sihui is only a short trip from prosperous Hong

Kong and its many rich customers. Within a short time a thriving jadeite market was operating with a daily stream of visitors from across the border. When Hong Kong was handed back to China by the British in 1997 things really took off.

Soon there were not enough craftsmen to keep up with demand. Wood and marble carvers from nearby Fujian province poured into Sihui and began to fashion jade instead. Carvers arrived from other provinces to share in this sudden new wealth. Even the jade carvers who worked in Canton Road in Hong Kong picked up their tools and moved to the mainland.

Sihui grew and grew. By about 2010 it had changed from a sleepy town with a small jade industry and a few hundred workers into a small, bustling city with a jade industry employing more than one hundred and fifty thousand people.

Seventy percent of all the jadeite carved in China comes from Sihui. More than seven thousand tons is used each year to fashion pieces big and small. Nearly all large jadeite carvings, some weighing tons, originate there. If you buy a jadeite pendant anywhere in China, or around the world for that matter, it very likely comes from this city. These can vary from pendants in the brilliant kingfisher green jadeite set in white gold and a coruscation of diamonds costing from US$10,000 to US$100,000, to simple computer-carved pieces costing US$20 or so.

Originally most of the jadeite fashioned in the workshops of Sihui was sold at one early-morning market. Now demand is so high that there are a series of markets. The two largest, the Daylight Market (*tian guang xu)* and the Market of Abundant Prosperity (*wan xing long)* are open twenty-four hours a day. Vendors come in three shifts: the dawn shift starts at about four a.m, the day shift at ten and the evening shift which starts about six and stretches into the early hours of the next morning. Millions of dollars in sales are made daily.

JADEITE CARVING CENTERS

All the centers for jadeite are concentrated in the two southern provinces of Guangdong and Yunnan. Guangdong is by far the largest producer of the two. Not only are there one hundred and fifty thousand people in Sihui but there are also twenty thousand people in the Pingzhou district of the city of Foshan where they specialize in bangles. You can almost guarantee that any jadeite bangle you buy is carved there. Ten thousand more work in the city of Jieyang where they concentrate on very high-end jadeite carvings. For some strange reason there is also a small hub of carvers who specialize in green nephrite.

A lot of jadeite is also worked in Yunnan. This province shares a border with Myanmar where the jadeite mines are situated and there are thriving markets in the border town of Ruili where twenty thousand people are involved in the trade. Thousands more make a living from jadeite in Yingjiang which specializes in the sale of rough uncut boulders. Mangshi and Lijiang also have thousands of people who work with jadeite.

A small jade industry has also sprung up in Fujian province, on the coast opposite Taiwan. Some of the wood and marble carvers who moved to Sihui in the 1990s and adapted their skills to carving jadeite have since returned home and set up business there.

There are many stories which are told about the original early morning market, in Sihui. Some still talk about Chinese merchants, hands hidden inside long silk sleeves, using a secret finger language to bargain over the price of jade. Others tell of how merchants would arrive before dawn, buy jades and then take a ferry to Hong Kong to sell them before lunch time on Canton Road for an immediate and very handsome profit.

There is no doubt these things happened in the past, but they are now distant memories. My experience of the jade markets in Sihui is very different. When I first went there a few years ago, I was woken up bleary-eyed at four in the morning to be taken to the Daylight Market. We traveled in a car through silent streets to the market then walked inside to be hit by a wall of noise. It was a vast covered area with thousands of people buying and selling and haggling loudly over price.

The lighting was always very dim, and I was always fortunate enough to be chaperoned by an expert carver who stopped me from making extravagant purchases. On my first trip. I found a pair of piglets carved in lavender jadeite which looked exquisite and seemed very reasonably priced. My friend pulled out his torch and proceeded to show me the slight flaws in the jade and variations in color which made them almost worthless.

I didn't buy the piglets but always enjoyed the hustle and bustle of Tian Guang Xu. It's a pity that it has to a large extent faded into memory. In just a few short years, the advance of technology means a lot of traders from all over China no longer bother to go to Sihui to buy their jade and the markets no longer have the same sense of hurly-burly and smell of money exchanging hands.

Most of the deals are now done online, as are the payments. Why would a merchant travel across the country to buy jades if he can view them on the Internet, agree a price and have them delivered by courier the next day? Especially if the person they talk to online is someone they already know and trust? The system works beautifully for those who are in the trade. They know what they want, have a good idea of price and there is a 48-hour return policy if the jade is not up to scratch.

Tian Guang Xu has now metamorphosed into a huge maze of retail outlets. They each seem muted with the customers thinly spread doing minimal business, but this could not be further from the truth. People may not be there in person, but at any one time thousands if not tens of thousands of people are viewing the jades live online. This is where middlemen - actually its almost always women - with their own customer bases walk around the market showing their clients what is on offer in a private channel broadcast from a mobile phone.

The *zhi bo* (streaming) agents often have assistants who use the phone to film the agent walking around the market talking to the merchants and chatting about all things jade. If one of the thousands of online customers sees a piece they like, then the agent haggles on their behalf. The assistant will then take the order and sort out payment.

It's great live television and Chinese people love it. They can be sitting at their desk at work or be at home doing the cooking with half an eye on the broadcast on their mobile phone. It is now estimated that a third of all sales in the Sihui jade markets are made in this way and I am told business is booming. The *zhi bo* agent makes money by takings a ten per cent commission from the seller. A good agent makes thousands of dollars a month doing this. When I last enquired, there were more than 3,000 *zhi bo* agents making a living in Sihui. They sprang up almost overnight - in the summer of 2017 there were none. When I next visited in 2018, they were all over the place, and it's a system which is now spreading throughout the country.

The very best agents don't even bother walking round the markets. They rent their own booths from which they broadcast live and jade carvers eager for sales queue up to go on air with these "Super Agents." The craftsmen can sell more this way in an hour than they used to sell in a month. It's a great system. I am currently in negotiations with one to do a monthly broadcast from my gallery in Suzhou.

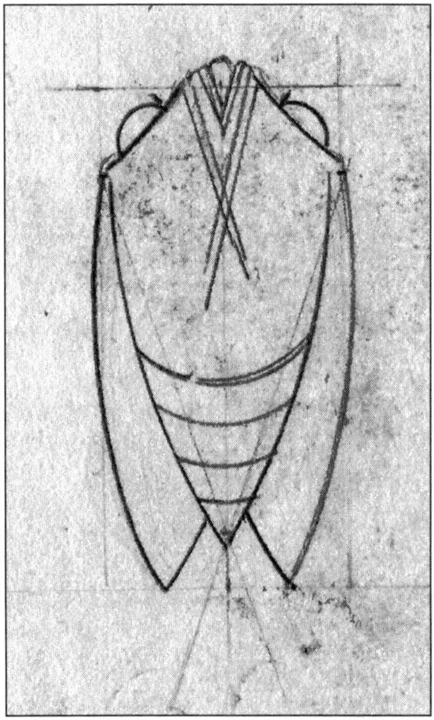

6

Nephrite Carving Centers

In the center of China, in the most ancient part of the Middle Kingdom, is The Temple of the Stone Buddha, a huge wholesale jade market in Zhenping in Henan province. When I need supplies of rough jade for my workshop I usually travel there to buy them. My wife hates me going there. She says the people of

Henan are not to be trusted. But I love it.

It is not an easy place to get to. The bullet train stops about two hundred kilometers away in the provincial capital of Zhengzhou and then it's a bumpy three-hour bus ride. There is one flight every evening from Shanghai which arrives shortly before midnight in the much-closer city of Nanyang and taxi drivers are then delighted to drive me more than fifty kilometers to the Temple of the Stone Buddha for an exorbitant fare.

I always check into the All Birds Make Obeisance to the Phoenix Hotel on the approach to the Temple of the Stone Buddha. I have never been able to find this temple, by the way. Ask people where it is and they shrug and say it is lost in the mists of time. But they can readily point you in the right direction to buy whatever jade product you want.

There is street after street of shops selling jade of every description, thousands of workshops carving beads, necklaces, pendants, bangles, lighters, cabochons, teapots, cups, vases, figurines, Bi discs and almost anything you can imagine made of jade. There are covered markets the size of aircraft hangars with a thousand stalls in each and the streets between the markets are packed with stalls where more of the same is on offer. There are entire roads of small businesses which have rooms full of computer-controlled machinery carving jade. There are tiny alleys full of one-room dwellings with a craftsman, his spindle, his bed and an electric ring to cook food on. You can stumble across windowless rooms crammed with young women sanding and polishing jade.

There are those who specialize in etching sigils and Chinese characters into the stone for use as chops. Goldsmiths set jade with precious metals and gems. There are shops which specialize in jade beads, and other tiny establishments string the finished carvings so they can be worn by customers. There are shops that sell all the tools carvers need for their craft. Almost everything you could possibly need or want in connection with carving is here.

There are also open-air and covered markets with thousands of tons of uncut nephrite for sale. Craftsmen come from all over China to buy it. Three of these markets are within a stone's throw of All Birds Make Obeisance to the Phoenix Hotel. It is one of the two reasons I stay there. The other reason is because I have little choice. It is one of only three hotels in the town where foreigners are allowed to check in. The hotel is not just for foreign guests, of course. If it was, it would go out of business. On most of my visits, I don't see any other non-Chinese at the hotel, in the restaurants or in the markets.

The first of the three markets near to my hotel doesn't start until mid-morning but I always get up early, wolf down a breakfast of steamed buns, tofu and rice porridge then squeeze into one of the tiny, bright red electric cabs and head for the early-morning New Town Jade Market a few kilometers away. It's held in a large open square about 200 meters by 200 meters and specializes in Russian, Korean and Qinghai jade. The best deals are on offer as the market is just opening at seven o'clock. A few vendors usually have some small pieces of good quality Korean jade laid out on the back of their small electric carts on the edge of the square. Furious haggling takes place and these sellers are usually gone before the market really gets going. I have never been able to find out where they get their jade to sell but have a gut feeling the jades are offcuts from some of the workshops which make larger pieces such as vases, bangles and teapots.

There are hundreds of vendors and tons of rough jade on sale from slivers smaller than a little finger to boulders weighing hundreds of kilos. By eight in the morning the market is packed with people. The best on sale is the white Siberian. Next down the line is Qinghai jade and bottom of the ladder is Korean jade. Most of the Korean on sale is a sweet celadon color but it's not worth much. I always come here for the white Siberian. The same jade in Suzhou costs me three times as much.

After a couple of hours at this market, I return to the hotel and drop off any purchases then walk about one hundred and fifty meters down an alley to a covered market where Uighur merchants from Xinjiang province sell the fabled Hetian jade.

There is no sign or indication on the outside to let you know that the market exists. There are two small entrances. Go in either door, pass through a metal detector and you are hit by a wall of noise as merchants and customers haggle over stone. The metal detector is there because arguments over jade can get quite heated and Uighurs by tradition carry knives. Old habits die hard.

It's a small market with only two hundred and fifty stalls. Craftsmen are keen to get hold of any good-quality white Hetian seed jade but it is becoming rarer and rarer and very little of it reaches a market like this one. When I first started my yearly buying trips, there was still some available but now the market is full of the lower-quality white jade from Qiemo in the Kunlun Mountains. I usually pick up a few pebbles of this, then dive into a nearby noodle bar for lunch.

I spend the afternoon in the other two markets near to my hotel. Some of the vendors are the same as those who sell jade in the early morning market. They pack up at lunchtime and move to the afternoon market in search of new customers. This is a good thing for me. It lets the merchants know that I am looking around before buying and gives me a chance to get to know them. I often don't buy much until my last day, by which time the prices have usually come down considerably. My best purchases are usually made just before I leave. By that time I have been chatting with a few of the merchants for a while and producing a wad of notes from my pocket at the last minute often does the trick.

I usually deal with women rather than men. This is because men seem to think they have to get a higher price from a foreigner than from a Chinese person and they want other stall-holders to see how easily they can trick the *lao wai* – to the extent that they will refuse to sell to me at a realistic price. Women, on the other hand, seem far more pragmatic and willing to do business.

A full day of trudging round markets leaves me exhausted. I return to the hotel about four and collapse on to my bed for an afternoon nap before thinking ahead to dinner. The markets are closed in the evening so it is time to eat, drink and make merry. The restaurants have tables full of men and loud laughter. They drink beer and copious amounts of *bai jiu* - a Chinese spirit which is more popular than whiskey is in the West - compare notes on market prices and that day's purchases, swap stories and let their hair down a little. It may be a business trip but the evening is a time to relax and have fun.

There's also a serious side to it. Deals are struck as merchants wine and dine customers in the many restaurants. The other guests at my hotel are all in the jade business, but they are not all carvers. Some own shops that sell jade. I bumped into one I knew on my last trip who had just bought fifty bangles.

He had purchased thirty bangles made from a sweet white Qinghai jade and twenty slim bangles in a pleasant green color. They cost him a total of about US$50,000, and over the next twelve months he was going to sell them all and treble his money. They weren't carved from the highly sought-after mutton fat white jade from Hetian, but then not everyone can afford to buy such a bangle. One bangle in decent Hetian jade would cost as much as he had paid for thirty good white bangles from Qinghai.

The jade merchant I bumped into is a canny man and not

easily fooled into parting with his money for shoddy goods. I jokingly asked him where he had purchased his bangles knowing that he was never going to tell me. He did offer to sell them to me at what he told me was the very fair markup of twenty per cent. It wasn't a bad deal. They were good-quality bangles and as a foreigner I would have had difficulty getting the same price. But I passed on the opportunity. Too much trouble retailing them.

Traders and carvers who stay at the hotels like All Birds Make Obeisance to the Phoenix usually have contacts and relationships with wholesalers. They don't usually trawl through the markets in search of a bargain. As regular customers who buy in bulk, they get preferential treatment. The merchants often come to them.

Less successful businessmen and poorer carvers endure a cheap and uncomfortable overnight bus journey to get to the markets. They arrive in the morning so they can immediately begin to search for the jade they want. Lunch is a hurried affair at one of the many cheap canteens that cater to the thousands of people who visit the markets every day. These buyers usually stay at one of the small inns or hostels which cost a few dollars a night.

Craftsmen often travel together. They can cover more ground as a team and if some choice stone is on offer that one person can't afford, they can pool resources to buy it. It's always a group of family members and close friends. They keep things very close in China.

The Temple of the Stone Buddha is by far the largest center for nephrite jade in China. As many people work with jade here as do in the main Jadeite center in Sihui in Guangdong Province.

Nearby provinces also have tens of thousands working with jade. Anhui has three places which are carving hubs, the best known of which is the city of Bengbu in the north of the province. It is famous for mass-produced reproductions and fake antique jade. Some are very high-end copies and are sold at reputable auction houses around China as the real thing. Mass-produced reproductions from Bengbu can be bought at antique markets and emporiums all over the country. Some say that sixty thousand people work in its five carving districts. I think this is an exaggeration. There are four thousand workshops in Bengbu but there are not fifteen people working in each one. I think it is probably fairer to say that the combined jade workforce in Anhui province is close to sixty thousand.

There are also thousands of jade workers in the provinces of Shandong, Guangxi and Qinghai. The mega cities of Shanghai and Beijing are home to many extremely gifted carvers and artists who have settled there because it is where they can command very high prices for their work. Wherever you go in China, whichever town, city or province, there will be someone either carving or selling jade.

Jiangsu Province to the west of Shanghai has three cities where tens of thousands of people work with jade. There is Yangzhou, which has a long and noble tradition of carving and a nationwide reputation for crafting large pieces sometimes weighing more than a ton. It is perhaps the only city where one of the factories set up under Mao still survives. There is Xuzhou in northern Jiangsu, a huge, sprawling, polluted city where thousands more work with stone. This is not to be confused with the the jewel in the crown, Suzhou, where I practice my craft. Suzhou is famous for its superb carvings in white Hetian jade, many of which are done in the style of the Ming and Qing Dynasties.

Wherever you go in Suzhou and its surrounds, you will come across jade, sometimes in surprising places. There is one tiny little village sixty kilometers away which only exists to make exquisite tea pots, cups, perfume bottles and vases. Only one bus goes to the village. It stops there four times a day.

I am biased in favor of Suzhou because it is the city which I call home but there is no doubt that the skill levels of the master carvers here know no equal in China or the world. I spent some of the happiest years of my life studying in the main jade carving district. I met my wife in Suzhou. My workshop and many friends are in the city.

Suzhou is a major tourist destination for Chinese people. The city's tourist board tell me more than a million visitors a month. It is considered one of the two most beautiful cities in the country. There is even a saying which goes something along the lines of "Above there is heaven and below there is Suzhou and Hangzhou" – *shang you tian tang xia you su hang*.

Unfortunately the beauty these visitors are seeking has virtually disappeared. The tree-lined boulevards of the city are no more. Its hundreds of canals are hidden away behind office blocks and apartment complexes. Its magnificent classical Chinese gardens which used to exude harmony and peace are now jammed with large groups of tourists pushing, shoving and shouting at each other as they take selfies.

You can still find glimmers of the tranquility and beauty that Suzhou was once so famous for. You can still find clues as to why Mandarins from the imperial court would retire here to wile away their final years. Walk inside the arts and crafts museum on *xibei jie*, for example, and you are transported from the noise of street sellers and honking cars into the peace and quiet of an old eighteenth-century mansion with its little gardens and rooms lined with rosewood and filled with cultural treasures.

Or try the Ming Dynasty mansion that houses the Opera Museum in Pingjiang. An oasis of quiet where I often used to go to do my Chinese homework. It's down a little alley only yards from a famous street jam packed with thousands of tourists. Few of them notice it tucked away just off the beaten path. It has the added attraction that on certain days you might catch the singers rehearsing. It's a funny old world. The only time I have come across openly gay men in Suzhou are those performing in the opera or selling flowers.

But places like the Opera Museum are just glimpses of an idealized past, Suzhou today is a crowded, raucous city bursting with life and energy. Chinese people talk of "the hundred years of humiliation" as the century when the Western powers (and Japan) inflicted defeat after defeat and heaped humiliation after humiliation on China. But in Suzhou, jade carvers talk of "the hundred years of silence" when the spindles were no longer turning and jade wasn't being carved. This is a poetic rather than an accurate description of the period between the collapse of the Qing dynasty in 1911 and the re-emergence of jade craft in the last decade of the twentieth century. I like to think of the bustle and noise as a celebration of the end of that era of silence and shame. It's Suzhou's way of telling the world that it is yet again standing proud and will bow before no one.

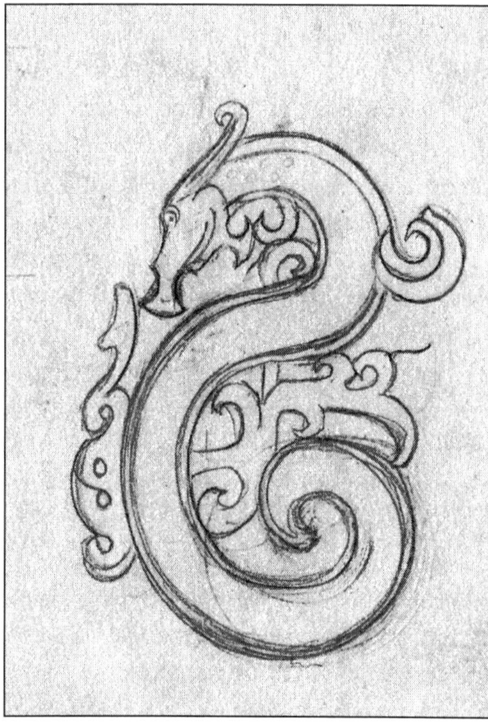

7

The Carving Process

I THINK OF CARVING as an eight-stage process. While there are no official guidelines on how to buy stone, carve it and sell it, I have my own thoughts on the matter:

Stage one: obtaining the stone

The first stage of the carving process is to obtain some stone. The easiest way to do this is for the craftsman to be given some jade by a customer who will pay him a set fee to carve something from it. Commissions like these are popular with carvers because they don't have to spend their own money on rough jade and are guaranteed payment. They are especially popular with young carvers who are just starting out and don't have much money.

The other way to obtain stone is to buy it. The most common way for young craftsmen to do this is to go to a jade market, but this is a very risky process. Nearly all the merchants who sell nephrite, for example, are Uighurs from the northwest of China and they are utterly ruthless businessmen. They dye the stone to hide the true color and the flaws within it. They treat it with chemicals to alter its appearance and make it seem more valuable. They try to pass off cheaper white Russian jade as more expensive Hetian River cobbles. It is common to see serpentine, treated glass and even plastic on sale as jade at the market.

The merchants' cunning knows no end. It is a popular practice for traders with good stock to lay out their stones on their black cloth and place one eye catching but far inferior stone in the center of their display in the hope that some unwary carver will be duped into thinking it is the same quality as the pebbles that surround it. Many a young carver has gone to the market with hard-earned money he has made from commissions only to walk away with jade that turns out to be virtually worthless, or worth far less than they paid for it.

There are also pitfalls to buying jadeite. Good jadeite is so valuable that very sophisticated techniques are now used to enhance the color. Even master carvers with years of experience in assessing jadeite have to send it to a lab to ensure that the jade and the color are genuine. There are workshops in Henan and Guangdong which specialize in transforming poor-quality jadeite into what appears to be good stone.

More established carvers with money in the bank are less likely to go to the markets and gamble in this way. They will have established relationships over the years with jade merchants and will phone them when they need stone. As regular customers they are less likely to be cheated. No-one wants to kill the goose that lays the golden egg.

A popular way for the larger workshops to reduce costs is to buy jade in large quantities. A hundred kilos of jade is far cheaper than buying by the kilo. Buying imported jade by the ton is also a favored option. I have a friend with one of the larger workshops which employs about twenty craftsmen and he buys two or three tons at a time. I know of purchases of this size he has made in China, Pakistan, Canada, Siberia and Yemen.

To the unpracticed eye a ton of jade might not look very much. It is a very dense stone. A boulder weighing a ton could fit under the average kitchen table. Of course when merchants buy several tons of jade it doesn't always come in such large pieces. At the market in Qiemo in northern China you can buy a ton of jade but the largest piece in the lot you buy might only be a hundred kilos. In Canada the boulders might be much bigger and weigh several tons.

How much can be used for carving also varies enormously. Jade from Pakistan for example is an excellent green color and ideal for jewelry but only about five percent is good enough to be carved. This is reflected in the price. Canadian material on the other hand is relatively more expensive even though it doesn't have quite the same color and translucency. This is because a far greater percentage can be used for carving.

There are no set prices. An experienced buyer will assess how much of the stone can be carved and factor that into the price he offers. The raw material is not the only cost. If they have their own workshop they have to take into account wages, rent, machinery, tools, utilities and marketing among other things. If they are buying from abroad they also have to take into account shipping costs and import tax which add significantly to the cost.

There was a time when merchants could fool Chinese customs officials the stone they were importing was extremely cheap and get away with paying very little duty. Customs are wise to this and now make their own assessment of the value and tax accordingly.

There is no doubt that independent carvers with limited funds get leaner pickings than master carvers and rich owners of large workshops. Most of the jade that reaches the markets is of poorer quality and has been treated in some way. Good jade is still available but the cost is far higher than buying in bulk.

Stage two: cutting the stone

Once a carver has bought some stone, whether nephrite or jadeite, the next stage is to rush to the jade cutter. These are experts in sawing jade into manageable pieces for carving. They know stone better than anyone else because they handle it every day. A steady stream of craftsmen visit them with stone they want cut open to see whether they have bought wisely or not. The cutters are witness to both anguish and delight.

Those who have bought jade sometimes find the stone they have paid a small fortune for is not quite as good inside once cut open. I know of one established carver with a large workshop who paid more than US$1,000,000 for a hunk of nephrite only to find when he sawed it open that he had bought stone of far inferior value. He had to let half his workforce go and move to smaller premises as a result.

Even master carvers defer to the cutters when it comes to

sawing up stone. The cutters have so much experience that they know better than anyone else how to divide a piece of jade to extract the maximum value from it. With jade so expensive that it is often paid for by the gram it is essential that every usable piece is fashioned into something that can be sold to make a profit.

The cutter himself will only make recommendations, he will not decide for you. Yet again this is because jade is so expensive he does not want to be blamed for any mistakes. He will use a pencil to draw lines on the jade where he suggests it may be cut but the final decision is always with the carver. I took the first large piece of white jade I bought to a master cutter and asked his advice. I deferred to his every decision and made far more from my purchase than if I had decided where to cut it myself.

Stage three: design

The third stage is design. Most craftsmen think of this as the most important part of the process. During my two years of study in the jade carving alleys under the direction of Wufan, I would often stop work and watch as he and his wife discussed with a customer how a piece of jade was to be carved.

The customer would enter and Wufan and his wife, Xiang Qin, would stand up wreathed in smiles of welcome. Cigarettes and green tea would be offered and after some polite chatter the rough stones would be produced for inspection.

Wufan, Xiang Qin and the customer would spend about half an hour discussing how best to carve these stones, which would vary from about twenty to a hundred grams in weight and could usually fit in the palm of your hand. This would include drawings in a sketchpad and designs being pencilled on to the stones, rubbed off and redrawn a number of times. Wufan always impressed on me that design is key to jade carving. It is said that a true Master is able to see the design in the stone before he carves it.

Good jade is so expensive that a carver doesn't want to buy a 30-gram pebble and end up with a 20-gram carving. With the best jade costing hundreds of dollars a gram it would be like throwing away money.

The oxidized skin of the stone, the shape, color, translucency, cracks, flaws and impurities all have to be taken into account. A good carver will incorporate these into the design. I have seen beautiful pieces designed around the different colors and even a crack in the stone. So a discussion about how to carve a jade is a serious matter.

There is a famous story about an emperor who was given a gift of a fabulous piece of jade which he wanted carved into a thing of beauty. The story goes something like this: He was so delighted with his gift that he immediately summoned the best craftsman in the land to carve it into two flying geese. The craftsman took away the jade and said he would do his best. After a year he had still not returned and the monarch summoned him and asked him where his jade was. The craftsman groveled on the floor and said it wasn't quite ready yet.

Another year passed and this time the emperor sent his soldiers to fetch the carver to demand an explanation for the delay. His soldiers returned not only with the carver but the stone he was meant to carve still untouched. In a fury the sovereign demanded an explanation. The carver tremblingly told him that he was very sorry but he didn't see two flying geese in the stone but a pair of carp swimming in a pond. The ruler was a wise man and gave the carver another chance. The craftsman returned a year later with a magnificent carving of fish swimming in a pool. The emperor was so pleased he showered him with gifts and forgave him.

I have no idea if this story is true and I have heard a number of versions of it, but carvers definitely put a lot of thought into the design process before even the first cut. During my time in Wufan's workshop, I once saw him place a fist-sized cobble of Hetian jade he had bought on the table next to his spindle and leave it there for about three months. Whenever I asked him why he hadn't yet carved it, he would always tell me without looking up "I am still thinking about it." He eventually fashioned an exquisite carving of a crab which made enough money to pay for six months' rent on his workshop.

Design is also extremely important in the larger workshops doing relatively mass production. A good design can be a real money spinner. If it is popular they might be able to sell hundreds of them. Often software is used to help design a piece in three dimensions, and nowadays it is common for many of these pieces to be carved or at least preformed by ever-more sophisticated machines operated by computers and then finished by hand. These jades are made from much less expensive stone than those used by individual craftsmen. The end-product is also much cheaper to buy. It is usually quite easy to tell whether a computer has been involved in the carving process as it will lack the soul and artistry of a jade fashioned by a true craftsman.

Stage four: carving

The fourth stage is the carving itself. In China, they think this is the easy bit. Once the stone has been bought and a design inked on to it, it is up to the carver just to follow the lines and fashion it to the required shape. Most carvers specialize in certain designs. Wufan has his own specialities which are flowers, birds and animals - mythical and real - in the style of the Qing dynasty. His brother-in-law, who he taught, is excellent at carving goldfish. People come to him for this reason. They can be confident that if they give him a stone and commission him to carve goldfish from it he will do a good job.

What the craftsmen do is not actually carving, although it has been called this for hundreds of years. You can carve wood and other materials but jade is just too tough to carve. Shaping it is achieved with slow and steady abrasion by materials even tougher than the jade. This usually involves diamond-plated or sintered diamond tools of various sizes. And patience. Lots of patience.

Everyone in China uses the same type of machine to carve jade. It has a long spindle with variable speed to which diamond coated tools are attached. They are very simple machines which seem to last forever. I have had mine for more than a decade. It is still going strong even though I have used it on most days for hours at a time. If it was a car, it would have done at least a million miles by now. There must be tens of thousands of these machines whirring away every day in China. For some reason, whichever factory produces them always paints them green.

There is some truth in the belief that carving is the easy bit. Apprentices are taught a set of techniques in their first two years which allow them to carve popular designs such as the Laughing Buddha, the Guanyin, various mythical animals like the *qilin* (Chinese unicorn), and real creatures such as horses and bats, as well as bamboo and flowers. What an apprentice usually concentrates on depends upon what his teacher specializes in.

The problem with this is that you can go into a thousand jade shops and the items they sell are almost identical. Each one has Buddhas, Guanyins, unicorns, flowers, goldfish, horses, bats etc on offer. There is very little originality, first because this is what every craftsman has been trained to carve and second because of customer demand. Jade carving is an ancient art and every carving has a meaning behind it. Customers often buy a specific design at the birth of a child, to wish someone success in exams or to give as a gift at a wedding. There are designs for each of these and many other occasions.

Originality in design is a rare thing in China. It is what separates the craftsman from the true master. A true master can design a Buddha which both conforms to the standard requirement and also seems fresh and original and then make it a reality with his superior technique. It takes a sort of genius to be able to do this. After all, the common designs which customers want to buy have been around for hundreds if not thousands of years.

And craftsmen are desperate for new ideas. Once a master has come up with a new design and put it on display in his shop it will be copied immediately. It is a bit like high street shops doing versions of the latest designer clothing seen on the catwalk at international fashion shows.

In my early days, I would often be approached by carvers who knew that I was on good terms with some of the masters and they would ask me to take photos of the latest designs in their workshops so they could get a head start. I would pretend not to understand.

One design I introduced to China, known as the Triple Möbius, has now been copied and is churned out by the thousand every week by factories in Henan and Guangdong. They do a far inferior version to mine with much cheaper stone using computers and it is sold at a price I cannot match.

Stages five and six: sanding and polishing

Sanding and polishing are usually done in the same workshop even though they are two distinct processes. They are skills separate from carving and done by different craftsmen and women. Sanding takes time, patience, very keen eyesight, extremely bright lights and an attention to detail that escapes many people.

The diamond-plated tools that are needed to carve jade leave marks and grooves which have to be smoothed out. Each sanding and polishing workshop has its own methods to do this but they usually follow a set pattern. An abrasive called silicon carbide is used to smooth out the bumps and divots left by the diamond tools. Workers start with a coarse grit and will then move on to ever finer grits to make the jade ever smoother.

Often you will find workers sitting in a row under very bright lights. Each person will do one stage of the sanding. The first worker will sand it smooth with a very coarse grit. The next will use a slightly finer grit and so on until it is smooth to the touch and any tool marks have been ground away.

Sometimes coarse diamond power mixed with vaseline or some other medium is used instead of silicone carbide. There are many methods and sometimes different grits are used on different types of jade. Jade is a rock, and no two rocks are quite the same. Sometimes it takes a very experienced sander to get it just right.

These workshops won't accept a carving if they don't think it is ready for sanding. If they decide the grooves and ruts caused by the diamond tools are too rough they will hand the jade back and tell the craftsman to bring it back when he has finished it. When I first started, I was told this on numerous occasions. It made me really focus on my carving. It often doubled the time it took for me to finish one piece.

After the jade has been sanded smooth it is ready to polish. There are different polishes available. Some of them suit white jade, while some of them suit jades of other colors. Each workshop has its own preferences and there are different finishes. Some prefer a matt finish and others prefer a sharper finish. But the end product should always look beautiful and flawless to someone with 20/20 vision.

There are many tricks of the trade to improve the look of a jade once polished. Sometimes a crack will occur or become apparent during the carving process. The most common method of dealing with this is to place the jade in a bowl of warm wax or olive oil for a couple of days. The wax or oil will fill the crack and make it imperceptible to the naked eye.

Most of the sanding and polishing is done by young women with sharp eyesight and attention to detail. There are some men who do this work too, but not many. Most of the carving is done by men. Again, there are some female craftsmen but not too many. This is a change from the time when carving was done in government-run factories. For some reason there were a lot more female carvers thirty years ago.

Stage seven: display

The seventh stage in the carving process is display. Once the jade has been finished it has to be put on show to catch the eye of prospective buyers. When I first came to Suzhou, very few craftsmen bothered with beautiful displays. There were two reasons for this, the first being that they would have to lay out a lot of cash on lighting and expensive cabinets which would attract the attention of their landlords and a hike in rent would soon follow. As a result, most workshops in the alleys were pretty squalid places with stone floors, peeling walls, a naked light bulb and a rickety old display cabinet to show the jades.

The second reason was that at that time, their customers didn't really worry about ambience. They were mainly trade and knew the value of a piece and would not be charmed or influenced by soft lighting showing the product in the best light.

This has all changed. When craftsmen open a new shop or refurbish an existing one, they now include display cabinets and lighting in the designs. Some even have fish ponds and tinkling fountains to create the right atmosphere.

There are now specialist carpentry shops where display stands in rosewood and mahogany, both large and small, can be commissioned in order to show jades in the best light. And if a young carver's pockets are not deep enough to commission these, they can be bought off-the-shelf in one of the stores that have opened just to cater to this need.

Pendants, bracelets, necklaces and girdle pieces (which are hung from the belt) also have to be strung on cords which can be silk, cotton, nylon or a mixture of these materials. There are shops where experts take a finished jade and string it to order. Hundreds of different cords in every color you can imagine are available, often complemented by beads of silver or semi-precious stones.

Stage eight: sales (haggling)

The eighth and final stage is to sell the finished product. The casual browser or the serious collector doesn't usually care how much money, effort and thought has gone into turning a raw piece of jade into a polished piece of great beauty. As they stroll around the best jade shops in the poshest malls and admire the handiwork of master carvers and jobbing artisans, their main focus once they have decided to buy is how much they will pay.

This is where haggling comes in. It doesn't matter if it's a small workshop, a posh mall or the gallery of one of the great masters, there will always be a negotiation over price. Chinese people love haggling. They are delighted at the thought of a discount or a bargain. Gleeful, even.

Sometimes a discussion over price can be quite loud and even alarming to Westerners. The first time I witnessed it was soon after I began learning my craft in Wufan's workshop. A thin man with a face sharp like a knife squeezed into the workshop one day just after lunch. He sat down and started talking to Wufan and asked to see some jades. He was a first-time customer and after it became clear he was a serious buyer, tea and cigarettes were offered.

He handled a few carvings, asked about prices then went back to chatting with Wufan. After about an hour he offered to buy a very nice pendant in white Hetian jade of a dragon with a rat. A piece carved in this way represents the hope that your son will become a dragon i.e. a great success in life. It is sometimes given to a young couple who have just had a son.

The price he offered was ridiculously low and Wufan refused point blank. He wasn't rude about it. He was quite pleasant but very loud in his insistence that the piece was worth at least four times as much as the man had offered. A half hour of very loud conversation followed which anywhere in my country, England, would have been considered a full-blown argument.

The jade was examined minutely by the customer and imagined flaws in the stone pointed out to Wufan. Then Wufan's wife became involved in the conversation and there even seemed to be a tug of war between her and the customer as they wrestled with the jade. At one point the customer seemed to pull her out of the workshop and then she dragged him back in. In the end a price was agreed and there were smiles all round.

There is a usually a minimum price in the mind of every craftsman when it comes to selling his jades. In Suzhou, an ordinary carver will expect at least a net profit of 20%. Canny buyers who understand stone can usually work out the bottom line. So, for example, if a customer sees a carving in good white Hetian seed jade weighing thirty-five grams he just needs to work out the cost of the raw stone, factor in the overheads such as labour, tools, rent and electricity, then add 20%. Its not an easy skill to acquire though. They say there are a thousand shades of white jade and each shade is of different value. Master carvers expect a far greater return than ordinary craftsmen. They usually work on the basis of 40% profit

The further down the scale you go the slimmer the margins. A workshop that concentrates on mass produced computer carved pieces using far less expensive stone will make a very small net profit per piece but will sell far more.

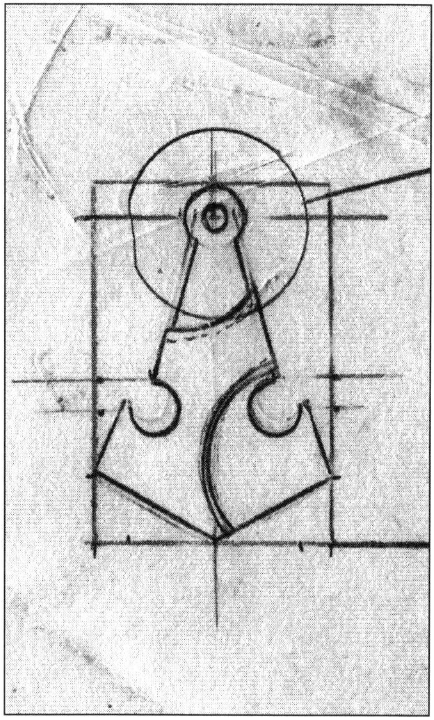

8

MASTER CARVER

QU LIJUN was a young man when he began working in the Suzhou factory in the late 1980s. He got the job after three years studying jade carving at Suzhou's Arts and Crafts College. He would cycle to the state-owned factory every day and work under the direction of older carvers. Even then, he stood out as someone with great talent. He was a tall and elegant man with the slender fingers of the true artist and a deep, mellow voice that people listened to. Ever courteous and thoughtful, he was well-liked by his colleagues and management thought highly of his work.

Then one day in February 1991, Qu Lijun stood up from his workbench and walked out of the door never to return. As a craftsman and artist he was fed up earning a pittance while the factory raked in large sums in valuable foreign currency from his work.

As far as he was concerned, the Suzhou state collective was part of the past. There were eighty carvers there producing jades, but their work supported sixty managers, a hundred and fifty other workers such as cleaners, security guards, cooks, salesmen, laundry workers *and* more than fifty retired craftsmen who still took a wage.

Qu Lijun had sat hunched over his spindle and watched out of the corner of his eye as rich foreign tourists strutted around the factory pointing at the pieces they wanted to purchase. He was paid just fifty cents a day for his skills and knew these buyers paid more than he would earn in a year for a piece that he had worked on for only a week or two. He wanted a bigger slice of the pie, felt he could do far better on his own.

Times were changing. Deng Xiaoping had opened China up to the global market and unleashed a revolution that was transforming the country into the economic powerhouse it is today. Getting rich was no longer a sin. Qu Lijun wanted to embrace the new order, carve in his own style and make money. His mind was brimming with new ideas and ways of working. Once free of the shackles of state management he felt could give free rein to his talent and perhaps get rich.

His work was already sought after by buyers, especially those from Taiwan and Hong Kong, who understood jade and appreciated his skill. Whispered conversations with these customers in darkened corners away from the prying eyes of management made it clear that if he branched out on his own there would be a steady stream of work.

One of his fellow workers was a pretty young girl called Liu Hongfang. They had fallen in love while studying jade carving at the Arts and Crafts college. After considerable discussion with her, he took the decision to leave the iron rice bowl certainty of the state-owned jade factory to start his own business.

Qu Lijun started looking for a place he could rent to set up his own workshop. He could have saved money and worked from home but ever-thoughtful, he didn't want to disturb his parents or his neighbors with the noise of his carving. Within weeks he had found a place in a single-storey building in Xiang Wang Alley in the southeast corner of the old city. He invited another carver to join him and took on two apprentices. It wasn't long before customers came knocking on his door.

During that first year, he froze in the winter and boiled in the summer as he worked on the commissions he was given. But he earned more than enough to pay the bills, and the quality of his work was so high that word began to spread and more customers came calling.

It wasn't just customers who came knocking at his door. Former colleagues popped by to see how he was doing. They liked what they saw. Within a year, half of them had walked out of their jobs at the factory to set up their own workshops. Most of them rented places in the same alley as Qu Lijun. After a year his girlfriend, Liu Hongfang, came to join him.

Within three years, all eighty carvers who worked at the factory had left and set up on their own. Most of them took on apprentices and rented places in Xiang Wang Alley. By 1994 there were more than fifty workshops with two hundred craftsmen and their apprentices selling to a growing number of customers.

As soon as the apprentices had done their two-year stint, they also set up in competition with their former teachers. They took on their own apprentices who in time would also set up workshops and so it went on.

People also set up as polishers and cutters. A shop began to sell carving tools. A couple of little canteens opened their doors to serve lunch to the workers. This was the beginning of the famous Jade Carving Alleys of Suzhou. Qu Lijun, however, had moved on. He rented better premises in another part of the city. He was well enough known and his work was of a high enough quality that his customers followed him.

China was changing fast and Suzhou was changing with it. The city began attracting a lot of foreign investment and huge factories began to spring up. Suzhou began to explode outwards. Workers began pouring in from all over China to get jobs on production lines. Some companies employed tens of thousands of people in what amounted to small private cities with dormitories, restaurants, supermarkets, hairdressers and little shops.

Suzhou was suddenly awash with cash. Some Chinese people were becoming very rich and looking to spend that money on luxuries. A few of them remembered their heritage and bought jade. Prices began to go up and by 1998 Qu Lijun, now known as Master Qu, began to make some real money. Not vast wealth, but enough for him and Liu Hongfang to marry, buy an apartment, start a family and – unheard of only five years before – purchase a car.

His reputation as a craftsman grew and grew. His work was considered so exquisite that he was increasingly sought out by rich collectors, corrupt government officials with black cash they needed to spend and the new fabulously rich entrepreneurs who had more money than they knew what to do with.

At the beginning of the twenty-first century, a national jade carving competition was launched where craftsmen could win medals and enhance their reputations. It was called *tian gong jiang,* which title translates as something like "The Work of Heaven." Master Qu became one of the first to be awarded a gold medal, and he won a number of others in the following years.

Meanwhile, Xiang Wang Alley continued to grow. Muslim jade merchants from the distant Xinjiang region set up a market to provide rough stone to the carvers. Only a few years before, they had been made to hand over boulders for pennies to communist officials from Beijing. Now they were free to travel thousands of miles to sell their stone at handsome prices to the carvers of Suzhou and other cities where jade carving was once again beginning to flourish.

Another street of jade shops opened near the Lion Forest Garden, a popular tourist destination. Other carvers set up in sight of Master Qu's new gallery and workshop, and jade malls sprang up in two or three locations in Suzhou. A small jade industry in the satellite town of Guangfu, set up years before with the help of craftsmen from Suzhou, began to mushroom. Little villages like Shandun and Yuli developed their own specialities and soon became reliant on jade for their prosperity.

Over the next few years there was a buying frenzy. The price of jade doubled, doubled again and then doubled yet again. Carvers couldn't keep up with demand and took on more apprentices. Even ordinary carvers began making enough money to buy cars.

Jades by Master Qu were now highly sought-after and commanded high prices, but he had not yet reached the pinnacle of his profession. To do that, he needed the coveted title of Chinese Jade Carving Master, something that was awarded to an elite few. To be eligible for this honor, a carver had to have been working for at least fifteen years. He could then submit three pieces of work which would be assessed by established masters on seven different criteria.

It was almost inevitable that he would be awarded the title, he just needed to be patient. Still a young man in his thirties, he would not even be eligible until the second half of the first decade of the new millennium. He attained the title in 2010. The rewards were enormous. Collectors paid more for a piece that came from the workshop of a master carver.

At the top of the tree, acknowledged masters such as Qu Lijun started to earn previously undreamed of amounts. A tea set for US$100,0000 or US$50,000 for a bangle in pure white jade, such prices were not uncommon.

Qu Lijun and Liu Hongfang have come a long way in less than three decades. He and his wife still go to the workshop every day, but he doesn't cycle, he now drives there in a Mercedes. She commutes to work in her Porsche. An elegant, attractive and cultured couple who work well together, they present just the right face to their well-heeled customers. She no longer carves but helps deal with important clients and takes a more administrative role. He still carves jade, which remains a passion, but he also has to supervise and direct his team of carvers. Master Qu only uses the very best Hetian jade – his reputation demands it – and needs to keep a close eye on the quality of the work his craftsmen produce.

When the family go on holiday, they usually go abroad. This year it's a month in Australia. Last year it was Thailand. Their son, who is a gifted artist, is now studying at one of London's top art colleges. Perhaps the next family holiday will be in London.

I knew none of this when I first met Master Qu twenty years after he set up the first workshop in Xiang Wang Alley. Until I heard his story, I thought the jade carving district with its little lanes was part of ancient Suzhou. I mistakenly believed craftsmen had been working there for hundreds of years. It never occurred to me that one young man had begun it by stepping away from the state-owned enterprise world and embracing the free market. And it all began because he decided that working in a government factory and earning a pittance was not for him.

Our first meeting was at a banquet following the opening of a major jade exhibition. I had just become the first foreigner to be invited to take part in such an event. I was pleased as punch to have been invited but felt a little lost sitting at a table with craftsmen I didn't know. Qu Lijun left the table of honor reserved for the acknowledged masters, came and sat next to me and started chatting.

At the end of the meal he gave me his card and invited me to visit him in his workshop. It was the beginning of a friendship which endures to this day. I began to seek him out on all matters relating to jade. One day I went to him for advice on what to do when my landlord decided to double the rent on my small workshop. Master Qu's response was to drive me in his Mercedes to another jade gallery he had about a mile away in a beautiful location and give me the second floor to use for as long as I wished, rent free. A spontaneous gesture that came from the heart.

And what happened to the old government factory where Qu Lijun began his career? It died a slow death. A core of diehard managers clung on for a few years after all the carvers had left. As its stock of jades ran out, they bought pieces wholesale to sell to its dwindling customer base. But the writing was on the wall, and in the late 1990s it closed its doors for the last time.

The same fate befell the other state-run jade factories. The only exception is the one in Yangzhou which is still operating although on a scale far below its glory days, when it had about six hundred workers. It specializes in sculpting jade boulders often weighing more than a ton, vases, tea sets, carved jade friezes and large sculptures of flowers, vegetables and fruit. This may well have helped it survive as it had the resources to buy the tons of jade needed to make things on such a large scale. During the 1990s and the early part of the twenty-first century it was commissioned to do two or three pieces a year weighing more than a ton. It would get hundreds of thousands of dollars for each piece and the profits helped keep it going. They still talk about the extremely high quality jadeite cabbage weighing one hundred and fifty kilos which sold for nearly US$2 million.

Unlike the other government collectives, Yangzhou streamlined itself after the reforms of Deng Xiaoping. It cut its workforce from six hundred to one hundred and signed contracts with companies in Taiwan and Hong Kong to supply them with jade. It also hired out its craftsmen to companies in Fujian and Shenzhen to train new carvers and manage the workshops that were springing up there. But the factory is now only a small part of Yangzhou's jade industry which today employs between ten and fifteen thousand people. It remains a leading player in the arts and crafts association but it is a shadow of its former self. Tastes have changed and commissions for sculpting huge boulders have shrunk to one a year at most. There are whispers that it is now running at a loss. A later edition of this book might well record its demise.

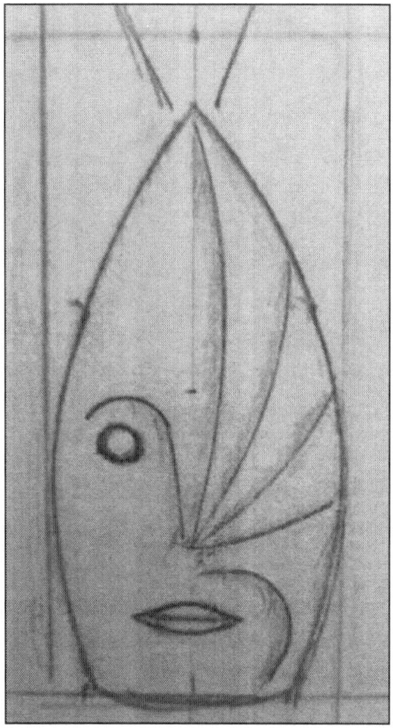

9

A Humble Craftsman

I will remain forever grateful to Wufan who taught me the basics of Chinese jade carving. He made space for me in his workshop, passed on his knowledge, allowed me to use a spindle every day, gave me old pieces of jade to practise on, encouraged me, welcomed me into his home and set me on the path to becoming a jade carver. This is his story.

Wufan was born in the city of Linyi in Shandong province in 1976 to a small shopkeeper and his wife. They already had three daughters, but like most Chinese couples they were very keen to have a son. China remains a very traditional society and boys are valued far more highly than girls. In those days, before China's one child policy, if the first-born was a girl, couples often continued to have children until a son appeared.

A stocky, boisterous boy, who often got himself into trouble, he was doted on by his parents and older sisters. After finishing school at the age of nineteen he earned money doing manual jobs without really knowing what he wanted to do, but he had expressed a passing interest in jade and his family started looking around for something suitable for him.

At the age of twenty-one, he was apprenticed to a jade carver in the city of Xuzhou in the neighboring province of Jiangsu. Apprenticeships are usually arranged through family connections. This job came about because the husband of one of Wufan's sisters knew a craftsman who needed help around his workshop.

Twenty-one is a late start for an apprentice but Wufan soon discovered a love of jade. Over the next twelve months, he learned a great deal about the basics of carving but things didn't work out. His teacher couldn't afford to keep him on. Wufan was out of a job.

He made his way down to Suzhou, where he had heard there were opportunities for a young man with talent and ambition in the rapidly expanding jade industry. He had no luck finding a job but undeterred continued on to the nearby town of Guangfu, which had developed a thriving industry of its own.

He found work cutting stone and pre-forming vases. He didn't carve the intricate detail which Chinese people love so much – that task was given to more experienced craftsmen. But by handling and cutting rough stone every day, he learned how to assess its value and how to tell good from bad.

By now, he had grown from a boisterous youth into a short, stocky man with an honest face and easy laugh. He worked hard and was well-liked by his boss. Wufan has a natural inborn courtesy which stands him in good stead in what remains a very deferential society. He liked this job and still looks back on it as one of the happiest times in his life. But after three years it was time to move on. There is no future in cutting stone for someone else.

With more experience under his belt, he managed to get a job as a carver in Suzhou's Xiang Wang Alley. He was still pretty raw but he had talent. He worked hard, earning a slightly higher wage and soaking up knowledge about jade carving and jade culture. After another three years, Wufan had developed a set of skills which was increasingly in demand. He was ready to move on again.

He got a job in one of the bigger workshops in another part of Suzhou and honed his skills even further. Within two years, he could carve almost anything but found that he had a particular talent for carving animals, birds and flowers in the traditional Chinese style.

As for most Chinese people, family is very important to Wufan. And like most Chinese people who leave their home town to seek their fortune, he rarely managed to get back home. He'd make his way back to Linyi to spend time with his parents and extended family of sisters, nieces, nephews, aunts, uncles and cousins but it wasn't a very satisfactory arrangement. So now that he was making a little bit more money, he asked his parents to come and join him.

Not long after this, a friend introduced him to a pretty and studious-looking young woman called Nie Xiangqin. There was an attraction between them and romance blossomed. He was a talented carver who wanted to open his own workshop and she had just graduated from art college and had a flair for design. It seemed a very good match. They married and Wufan left his job and opened his first tiny workshop in the alleys. It wasn't long before his wife was carving alongside him – Wufan passing on to her the skills that he had learned over the previous decade.

At first they had little money to buy jade and relied on commissions. Owners of jade shops would come with stone for them to carve. They soon gained a good reputation and got a steady stream of work. It was tough going and they had to scrimp and save just to pay the bills but whenever they had spare money Wufan would go to the jade market and buy stone he could carve himself.

His experience as a stone cutter helped tremendously. When he went to the market to buy jade he very rarely got cheated on stone or price. He remains one of the best judges of rough jade that I have met. A bad purchase can put a carver at the beginning of his career out of business.

After a couple of years not only did they have a steady stream of commissions but also a small cabinet of their own jades to offer customers. They moved to a bigger workshop, bought another jade carving machine and took on Xiangqin's brother as an apprentice.

The new workshop was about ten feet square. It had three dirty brick walls with peeling paint which might at one time have been white and a sliding glass door facing out on to the alley. Crammed into this small space were three electric spindles for carving jade, a glass case to display jade and a safe to store the carvings in at night. The floor was cold concrete. There was a tap in the corner to supply water.

The noise inside the workshop during working hours was deafening, with three machines spinning at the same time and the radio blaring away. Wufan didn't usually notice the screech of the drills or the raucous pop music. With his nose only inches from the spindle, shoulders hunched, neck thrust forward in total concentration and hands aching from holding the stone steady against the diamond coated burr hour after hour, he only had eyes for the jade in front of him. Carving jade requires total focus. He dared not blink under the glare of the powerful lamp shining on the stone in case his hand slipped and he made a mistake.

The only respite came when a customer showed an interest in a jade on display in the glass cabinet. Customers came and went all the time. They walked in but were ignored unless they wanted to buy. The prospect of a sale would bring carving to a halt.

Customers would come in, glance at each piece and then quite often walk out without saying a word. If they saw a piece they liked they might take it out of the shop into the sunlight to get a better look. If it pleased them they might make an offer on it. Furious haggling would ensue and perhaps a sale would be made.

Wufan is head of what is a typical modern Chinese family: husband, wife and one child along with the parents of the husband. It is usual for both the husband and wife to work while the grandparents look after the child. If you walk past the gates of a primary or junior school at the end of the day, you will see herds of grandparents who are responsible for the school run.

He is a generous soul and has never ceased to help his extended family. He has taught several of them to carve jade including his wife, her brother and a niece. They all now work in the alleys.

The next few years were good for Wufan. The 2008 Beijing

Olympics came and went. Jade became ever more popular. Prices continued to climb. He opened a shop in a prime position in a brand-new luxury jade mall. He also increased his prices. As the price of jade increased, so did the rents. Wufan had to move his workshop out of the alleys. A prime spot in Xiang Wang Alley now costs at least US$200 a square meter per month. Like many carvers, he now has his workshop in an apartment in a nearby housing complex. A stone's throw from the alleys, but much cheaper and with far more space.

He isn't there very often. He's in his forties now and mainly tends the shop in the luxury mall while others he has trained carve the jade for him. He doesn't want his son to follow him into the cutthroat world of jade carving. It's a tough business with a limited shelf life and an uncertain future. Profit margins are being squeezed year after year. Wufan wants to see his son go to university and gain a qualification that will mean a secure white collar job. He wants something better for his son than the daily grind of the jade spindle, in an ever more competitive market.

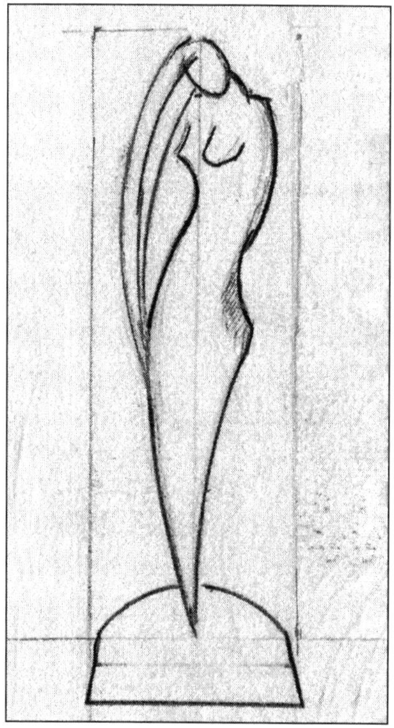

10

Jade Merchant

Green Jade Zhang is in his early fifties and looks like a great many men of his generation. He is short and thin, wears glasses, has black hair and dresses in a dark suit but never wears a tie. He does not stand out in a crowd and on first glance there seems to be nothing special about him. You might be mistaken in thinking he was just another of the millions of mid-level managers or businessmen working hard to put food on the table for his family. You would be wrong. Mr Zhang is the multi-millionaire owner of one of the largest jade workshops in China.

On the dashboard of his Audi he has placed the gold-braided hat of a colonel in the military police. Green Jade Zhang is not a policeman but having the hat in the car helps him to have trouble-free driving. It is a common practice for owners of expensive foreign cars to be victims of fraudsters who throw themselves in front of vehicles and then demand money in compensation for their imagined injuries. If the driver refuses, then the fraudster threatens to call the police. This is not something that any driver wants because under Chinese law the car driver is always at fault in an accident which involves a pedestrian, cyclist or electric bike. People who try this on Green Jade Zhang never try to extort money from him. Once they see the braided cap in his car they quickly make their excuses and leave. No one wants to mess with the military police.

Green Jade Zhang's real name is Zhang Jinhong. His nickname comes from the fact that he has managed to build up a multi-million dollar business in green nephrite in the city of Sihui in Guangdong province where everyone else carves jadeite. There are plenty of people in Sihui called Zhang who carve or sell jadeite. But there is only one man who deals in green nephrite so he's called Green Jade Zhang.

Everyone in Sihui knows who he is. He has brought fame and kudos to the city by erecting an imposing museum next to his factory to showcase green jades from around the world. It cost a fortune but he used his *guanxi* (personal networks) to get grants to help build it. He even managed to secure promises of money to help maintain it. The museum has given him huge face. There were plenty of jade workshops, markets and factories in Sihui but this is the only museum.

He traveled the country to buy antique jade carving tools and benches to display in the museum. Huge boulders of jade from Russia, Canada and New Zealand became exhibition pieces. A massive frieze in green jade and two jade vessels weighing a ton each have been placed in the entrance hall. Hundreds of carvings from around China and the world are housed in expensive display cases in three great halls. It was five years in the planning and building but when it was ready, the great and the good came from all over China to the opening. It was considered important enough to be featured on national television.

To coincide with the opening, he made a deal with the Miss Asia Beauty Pageant. Shortly after the museum opened, all the Miss Asia contestants were seen on TV wearing creations from his jade workshop. The pageant was beamed live to hundreds of millions all over Asia. The coverage helped boost sales of his jades throughout China.

It's all a far cry from his days studying chemistry at university in Guangzhou in the late 1980s. Even then, although still wet behind the ears, as it were, Zhang Jinhong was different. He wasn't sitting in his dormitory writing up his lecture notes at night. He was out and about trying to make friends with the strange foreigners who had begun to appear in Guangzhou.

These *lao wai* came to the universities as teachers and students, or as tourists or to do business. They fascinated Zhang Jinhong and he would go out every evening in search of their company. He spoke a little English learned in high school and this rapidly improved as he met and chatted with visitors from Europe, Australia, New Zealand and North America.

Slowly a plan began to develop. There were tens of thousands of people who wanted to learn English in Guangzhou. Premium prices were paid for lessons where you could chat to real foreigners and practice the English learned from books at school. Being able to speak English was a great advantage if you wanted to do business with a *lao wai* or get a well-paid job with one of the growing number of companies opening offices and factories in China.

Zhang Jinhong decided to open an English school staffed by foreign teachers. It was a great idea but to all his friends it seemed like an impossible dream. He had no money, no premises, no teachers and no chance of getting the all-important license needed for such an enterprise.

Zhang Jinhong was not to be put off. He was a great salesman, had a very sharp business brain and a flair for organization. He bribed three schools to let him use their empty classrooms in the evening. With the help of an airline pilot from New Zealand who he had befriended, he recruited foreigners studying at the university to teach classes.

He trawled the hotels where foreign tourists stayed and asked them to come to chat with his students. He found plenty of willing volunteers eager to meet ordinary Chinese people. He waited for tour buses to return to hotels after a day of sightseeing and once the guests were in the lobby would shout out, "Who wants to chat to some real Chinese people?" Half a dozen people would raise their hands and follow him to experience the real China. Very soon he had a thousand students enrolled in packed classes.

Zhang Jinhong, or Dracky, as he became known to his foreign friends, worked eighteen hours a day. After his university lectures he would work until the early hours of the morning organizing lessons, enrolling students, finding teachers and bribing the right people so that he could operate what was in effect an illegal school. He made so much money that after graduating he and his girlfriend decided to travel the world.

Dracky wanted to see the countries where all these strange foreigners had come from and find out if all the wonderful stories they told him were true. Not only was he a great businessman but he was also a dreamer. So in 1991, he and his girlfriend flew to New Zealand. His command of English and his salesmanship landed them both jobs with a Chinese company in Auckland.

In New Zealand he came across another business opportunity that was to change his travel plans and make him rich. He discovered that the "Greenstone" for which New Zealand was famous was in fact jade. He knew a little bit about jade because his older brother made a living as a carver in his home town of Sihui. Dracky watched as local people and tourists bought simple pendants for what, to his mind, were astronomical prices. He knew there was money to be made here, he just needed to work out how to cash in.

On a sightseeing trip to the town of Rotorua, he and his girlfriend walked into a little jade workshop and fell into conversation with the craftsman. There was an instant bond. By some strange twist of fate he had walked into the workshop of John Sheehan, the only American working as a jade carver in New Zealand. Both were strangers in a strange land. They were kindred spirits. Both had an eye for an opportunity. As John and Dracky chatted it soon became clear that labour and production costs in China were a tenth of what they were in New Zealand. Both men smelt money.

They went into partnership. John would buy a few kilos of Canadian jade from a wholesaler. Dracky would send it over to his brother to carve into Maori-style pendants. Each consignment that was sent back was sold at a handsome profit. It wasn't long before the finished jades coming back from China were far too numerous for John's shop to deal with. They started to wholesale to other outlets. No-one could match their prices. They didn't stop there. This was just the beginning. They knew they had stumbled on to a pot of gold but to develop the business they needed real money. They foresaw huge profits. But to make money they needed money and they didn't have enough. John Sheehan took a huge risk and remortgaged his house to raise the capital.

Now they had some real money, they bought jade direct from mines in British Columbia. They bought tons instead of kilos. A production line of thirty craftsmen in China were trained in the Kiwi style and fashioned Maori-style jades producing consignments of pendants, rings, bangles and the like, all shipped to New Zealand for sale.

Dracky and John were deeply unpopular with many in the jade carving world of New Zealand. They were taking a substantial share of the market and selling at prices local craftsmen couldn't compete with. People complained they were putting local carvers out of work. By the mid-1990s they had nine shops throughout the country. Two men, one from China and one from the United States had industrialized a small cottage industry.

It wasn't long before Dracky felt he was making enough money to buy a house and marry his long-time girlfriend. They became New Zealand citizens. Dracky, ever practical, realized that he could travel the world and do business far more easily with a New Zealand passport. He had come to New Zealand just to visit but had come to love it. Although a hard-headed businessman, he had also fallen in love with jade.

The next few years were hard work building up and consolidating the business. Dracky had boundless energy. John nicknamed him "The Energizer Bunny" after seeing a TV advert for a battery that claimed its product could go four times as long as normal batteries. The advert showed a toy bunny, powered by this battery, banging a drum long after similar toy bunnies using ordinary batteries had stopped moving. That was Dracky.

It didn't seem to matter how successful they were, Dracky worked tirelessly to make even more money. By the turn of the century, Dracky began to cast his eye towards the huge Chinese market. He was sure that the brand that he and John had built up over the years could be a success in the homeland of jade. If they could make a lot of money in a country with less than five million people, just think how much money they could make in a country of nearly one and a half billion where jade was a treasured possession.

John was persuaded by his arguments. They spent a lot of money promoting their brand in China. At first it was like throwing money away. After two years, without any sign of profits on the horizon, John pulled out. Dracky, on the other hand, persevered.

He knew it would take time to build up awareness of the brand and make significant sales. Chinese people are very wary of things they are not familiar with. There are so many scams in China that most people prefer to buy from a proven reputable source rather than risk something new.

As with most Chinese people, Dracky plays things very close to his chest. He doesn't talk about how much money he has or how much jade he sells but you can read between the lines. He buys tons of jade at a time, which is an indication that sales must be significant. When I last visited his factory, I admired the chains he uses to display his pendants. They are bronze chains washed with gold but they have a look, a heft and feel to them which is far superior to the ones I could buy elsewhere. I asked if he could perhaps sell me a couple of dozen and how much that would cost me. He shrugged and said he had no idea but he would check. He ordered his twenty thousand at a time he told me and had no idea how much he would charge me for so few.

Why do we both use fake gold chains to display our jades? Very simple. Every time a Chinese customer comes in, they will haggle over the price. Almost invariably they will want the chain thrown in at no extra cost. A bronze chain washed with gold might be a few dollars. A real gold chain is at least a hundred dollars.

Dracky never stops. Age has not slowed him down. His museum has been so successful that a consortium in Shandong province on the other side of China have signed a contract with him to construct a similar one in a theme park they are building. Last time he visited me in Suzhou, we traveled to a show in Yangzhou together and he then went on to Beijing for some high-level meetings of the Chinese Gem and Jewelry Association where he is on several committees. On his way back to his factory in Sihui he planned to visit the construction site in Shandong province where they were building the copycat museum. Hard work pays off. His brand of high quality green nephrite in both traditional Chinese and modern Western designs has truly achieved national recognition.

Dracky now owns homes in both China and New Zealand. He has plenty of staff and a chauffeur but still prefers to drive himself. He still works fifteen hours a day and rarely takes a break. Sometimes he grabs his golf clubs and walks to the driving range he has built behind his Jade Museum and hits a few balls. It's the nearest he gets to relaxation.

His son is studying business administration at a university in England. When I asked him what he wants his son to do, he laughs and says he doesn't want him to follow in his footsteps – jade is too much hard work. Dracky wants to give his son some of his own hard-earned cash and watch him use the business skills he learns at university to turn it into even more money – but from the comfort of an air-conditioned office and during regular business hours.

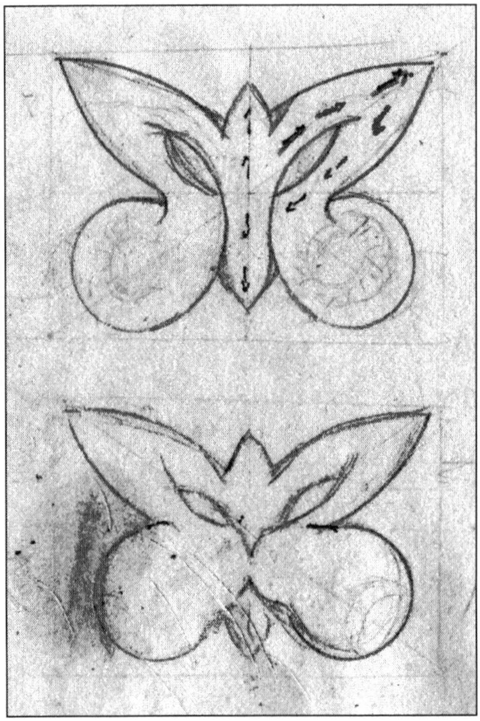

11

Symbolism in Jade Carving

When Westerners come to my gallery to buy jade, they are usually surprised that it comes in so many colors. Most of them think of jade as green. I love talking about jade, in fact it is difficult to shut me up, so I very quickly explain to them that it not only comes in a variety of colors but is also more than one type of stone.

Once they have accepted the idea that jade can be different colors they will then move on to how beautiful the design is. Design seems to be the overriding factor for a Western customer.

Chinese people are more interested in the quality of the stone. That is the first thing they think about, not the design. Those who love jade know that it is a precious commodity which is increasing in value all the time. A lot of Chinese people won't buy a piece just because they like the design, it has to be a good stone, and it has to have meaning. Most decent jades are carved with symbols which convey wishes for wealth, long life, luck, many children or success in exams.

Even poorly-educated Chinese people will rarely buy a jade pendant without knowing what it signifies. The waitresses at my teahouse and jade gallery in Suzhou are hard-working girls from the countryside. Whenever I display a new carving, the first thing they ask me is "What does it mean?"

Many carvings use homonyms to convey a message. Homonyms are words pronounced alike but having a different meaning. Examples in the English language include the words lead, as in the metal and led as in the past tense of the verb to lead, or the noun quail as in the bird or the verb quail as in to tremble. Or two, to and too.

The Chinese language is far more limited in sounds than English and there are far more homonyms, also because it is a monosyllabic language. Every word is one syllable and represented by one character. That means there are a huge number of homonyms in the language, and that provides all sorts of opportunities for wordplay.

An example is the word for the nocturnal flying creature, the bat. When I first came to China, I was surprised at the popularity of bats. They are looked on as omens of good fortune which is in direct contrast to the way they are viewed in the West through their association with vampires and cold dark caves. Even the superhero, Batman, is a threatening presence. In China, however, it has very positive connotations.

There are simple Chinese homonyms such as "*wu fu*" which translates as Five (*wu*) Bats (*fu*). But another character also with the pronunciation fu means "good fortune." So a carving of five bats represents the five traditional Chinese blessings of good health, a long life, wealth, love of virtue and a peaceful death in old age. Five Bats or Five Blessings – it sounds the same.

Because the word for "bat" is a homonym for "blessing", it has been associated with good luck for thousands of years. It is extremely important in jade carving. One lovely carving is a piece of bamboo with a bat clinging to it. The Chinese word for bamboo is *zhu,* and *zhu* can also mean, with another character, an expression of good wishes. So *zhu* means Bamboo and *fu* means Bat. So if you give this carving to a person as a gift it means you wish them good luck.

The common bottle-shaped gourd from the squash family is also viewed as a symbol of good luck and wealth. This is because the two characters in Chinese for the gourd sound very similar to those which mean good luck and prosperity. The god of long life, *shou xing,* carries a simple gourd which is said to hold the elixir of immortality. So a carving of *shou xing* carrying a gourd represents good luck, wealth AND long life.

Not only do most carvings have a meaning but there is usually a legend or folk tale behind them as well. A carving including, a peach, for example usually represents long life. This is because the peach is the fruit of immortality. The peach tree of the Gods is said to blossom once every three thousand years and produce the fruit of eternal life. So a peach and a bat together symbolize both good luck and long life.

A carving of a tortoise also represents longevity. This is

because tortoises live for a very long time but it is also a popular carving because it is one of the four sacred animals that appeared at the beginning of time to help the dwarf Pang Gu to create the world. The others being the dragon, the phoenix and the *qi lin*, a Chinese mythical beast similar to a unicorn.

The dragon and the phoenix are symbols of good luck. They are also seen as symbols of power. They have long been associated with the emperor and empress. But in more recent times, ordinary people have associated them with husband and wife. A pair of jades carved into a dragon and phoenix are popular wedding gifts. People mistakenly believe the two mythical animals are supposed to represent the bride and groom. This is not the case. They represent the idea that as they go through life together, they will become like the dragon and phoenix i.e. wise, powerful and benevolent.

A carving of a *qi lin* is often placed in the house of a couple who wish for a son. Legend has it that this mythical beast will only appear at the time of a good and wise ruler or a great man. One was said to have appeared shortly before the birth of Confucius and reappeared shortly before his death.

There are jade amulets purely to protect a person from harm. My favorite is a simple figure wearing flowing robes called Weng Zhong. The short version of the myth that surrounds him is that he was the personal bodyguard of the first emperor, Qin Shi Huang who ruled from 221-210 BC. Weng Zhong was said to be a master of Kung Fu, and when he died the emperor had a statue of him placed in front of his palace so that he could continue to protect him even after death.

The longer version tells of a child who by the age of ten was already six feet tall and enormously strong. He had such a huge appetite that by the time he was a teenager his family had difficulty feeding him. When the imperial army came recruiting, he signed up and soon gained a reputation as a fearsome warrior. His future was assured when he saved the emperor from an attack by a tiger. Legend has it that the emperor was walking in the forest deep in thought trying to work out strategies for his next military campaign when a tiger attacked. Weng Zhong leaped to his defense and killed the tiger. It was after this that the emperor made him his personal bodyguard. Not happy with being a simple bodyguard, Weng Zhong begged the emperor to let him lead his armies in a campaign against a fearsome tribe that was threatening the northwestern borders of the empire. It is said he had such prodigious strength that he threw the heavy Chinese spears into their ranks to kill them. Until this time the spear, was seen only as a weapon of hand-to-hand combat and never thrown. According to the myth he was so effective that his soldiers queued up to hand him their spears to throw and kill the enemy.

Legend also has it that at one point he pulled an enemy general from his horse and killed him, then ripped the horse into pieces with his bare hands and used the pieces to batter enemy soldiers to death. It is said that he was such a fearsome sight and personally slaughtered so many tribesmen that they were in mortal fear of him and worshipped him as a god.

In a variation of this myth, a single statue of him was not placed in front of the emperor's palace but instead several statues were placed on the wall that protected the borders of the empire as a warning of what would happen if the savages tried to invade again. This amulet is very popular with carvers because it is quite simple to make but has a certain beauty about it which appeals to buyers.

Another fierce warrior from four or five hundred years later, during the Three Kingdoms period in the third centuryA.D. called Guan Yu or Guan Di, is also a popular carving. This is far more ornate and shows a man with a flowing beard holding a spear. The two legendary warriors are often mistaken for each other. Guan Yu was a sworn brother of the emperor, Liu Bei, and utterly loyal to him. He symbolizes justice, dignity and loyalty, especially between friends. Deified in the Song dynasty as the Taoist god of war, he was later immortalized in *The Romance of the Three Kingdoms*, one of the four great classical novels of Chinese literature.

There is a carving known as *wu zi pai*, which literally translates as "No Words Tablet." This is a smooth piece of jade with no symbols or designs carved into its main body. The empty tablet, as it is also known, is left blank to express the wish that no disasters or troubles are written into the life of the recipient of such a gift. Because the *wu zi pai* represents the wish for a trouble-free life, the jade from which it is carved can have no defects.

There are jades which can be worn by anyone but have become popular gifts for children. They are usually amulets to ward off harm or to help ensure a long and happy life. A small circular disc with rounded edges and a hole in the middle is the most popular. It is called *ping an kou*. *Ping an* means safe and sound or without mishap, and the disc is something that it is believed will bring peace and safety to the wearer. A lucky charm. It is not to be confused with the ancient *bi* disc, which is entirely different.

Another popular gift for children is called *chang ming suo*, the literal translation of which is 'long life lock'. Used on doors and boxes, locks have a long association with protection from the unknown. Eventually, this idea transferred to the most precious thing in a parent's life, their children.

A variation of this is the *ping an suo* which is a cross between the *ping an kou* and a long life lock. This symbolizes not only protection from the unknown but also peace and safety.

Here is a selection of some of the other most common themes which you may see if you visit a jade shop in China.

Carp: The carp is a symbol of perseverance. It has long been associated with scholars, who needed great perseverance to succeed in the very tough imperial examinations. It is also associated with the myth of the carp turning into a dragon at the Dragon Gate Mountain. This myth likens the feat of scholars passing the civil service exam to the carp leaping untold heights and turning into a dragon, the most magnificent of all beasts.

Goldfish: A small member of the carp family. The Chinese word for goldfish, *jin yu,* is a homonym for gold and jade, representing wealth. the two words together are also a homonym for "gold in abundance" which means much the same thing.

Spider (and web): The meaning of a spider carved in jade is Joy from Heaven. This is because the Chinese words for spider is a homonym for joy. Joy comes from heaven and spiders also seem to drop from the sky.

Mandarin Ducks: Two mandarin ducks symbolize fidelity and marital bliss. They are invariably shown with a lotus. In this context, the lotus stands for harmony in marriage. An appropriate wedding gift.

Quail and rice: If you give someone a jade with a pair of quail and a rice plant with its ears of grain clearly carved on it, then it means you wish them peace year after year. This is yet another homonym. If the back of the jade is carved into the shape of a leaf, it has the added meaning of to live in peace and be happy in your work.

A Horse with a Monkey on its back: A traditional gift to express wishes for promotion.

Badger: Happiness. Two badgers: double happiness. A badger and magpie carved together also means double happiness.

Magpies: These are auspicious birds in China mainly due to the legend which surrounds the Chinese equivalent of Valentine's Day. The story, often called the Maiden and the Cowherd, is a tale of forbidden love and goes something like this: One of the daughters of the Goddess of Heaven came down to Earth one day and fell in love with a cowherd. They married and would have lived happily ever after except that when the Goddess found out she was furious and dragged her daughter back to heaven. The cowherd was bereft, but had no way of getting to heaven to be reunited with his wife. All the Magpies of the world took pity on the lovers and used their wings to form a bridge between Heaven and Earth so that they could meet, just once a year, on the seventh day of the seventh month (of the lunar calendar, which makes it in August). Hence the seventh day of the seventh month is now a day dedicated to romance. There are many versions of the story, but it is the magpies which are important in every one. They are seen as magical birds who are messengers of good news and happiness.

Boy on a fish: Best wishes for the family and success for the sons.

Lotus: The lotus has many meanings and more than one name in Chinese. A slice of lotus means a wish that every road you choose in life is trouble free. A lotus with fish in a pond means a wish that year after year you have wealth enough to get by. It is a also a wish for continuous good luck.

Goose: The goose is important because it denotes wealth. In the distant past, only nobles could afford to eat this bird because it was far more expensive than duck or chicken. Also a goose carved holding a ganoderma fungus in its beak means to have life as you wish it. This is because this type of fungus looks like the jade scepter or *ruyi* and the Chinese word for goose sounds very similar to the word for "I" or "me."

Buddha and Guanyin: Some will tell you that men should wear the Guanyin (a female Buddha) and women the Buddha, but this is propaganda put about by the monks in Buddhist temples who want to make money selling them. They are generally worn by Buddhists. But like the crucifix or cross in Western society and elsewhere, they are often worn as fashion accessories. Guanyin is considered to be the goddess of mercy and is venerated by Chinese Buddhists as the Bodhisattva of compassion. Her full name is *guan shi yin* which translates as one who hears all the cries of the world. She started out as male in India but seems to have had a sex change on the journey to China. She often wears a crown and sometimes an image of the Buddha is etched into that crown. This is just to show that she is just a little lower in the pecking order than the Buddha himself.

Last but not least is one of my favorites, the *pi xiu*, which is part lion and part dragon, has feathered wings, a very large mouth but no anus. One myth tells that it violated the law of heaven defecating on the floor of the jade palace. It was punished with a spanking executed by the Jade Emperor, and the spanking was hard enough to cause its rectum to be permanently sealed. The Jade Emperor further declared that the diet of the *pi xiu* would from then on be restricted to gold, silver and jewels. It can eat as much as it likes but it can never again defecate. The *pi xiu* is the symbol for the acquisition and preservation of wealth. A very popular carving in the new China where money is king.

I could bore you for hours with the different meanings and more stories behind these carvings but I won't.

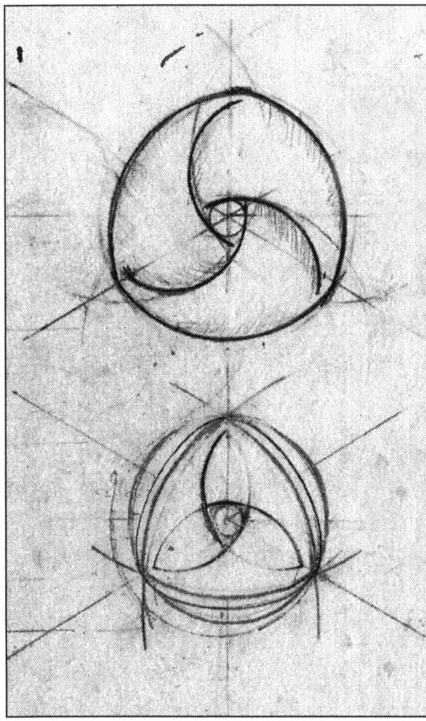

12

Fakes and Reproductions.

THERE IS ONE DAY in 1991 that Yao Shuming will never forget. He was in a good mood after a successful business trip where he had sold all but two of his jade carvings. That mood soured significantly when he was arrested by police at Xiamen railway station in the coastal province of Fujian as he was about to board a train back to Bengbu.

In a routine search of his luggage, officers had found what they thought were cultural relics. They didn't know much about ancient jades but they were pretty sure that what they discovered belonged in a museum rather than in Yao Shuming's suitcase.

Mr Yao protested his innocence. They were replicas, he told them. One was a copy of a jade from the neolithic Hongshan culture of more than five thousand years ago and the other from the Han Dynasty of two thousand years ago. He had carved them himself. He was a craftsman who specialized in carving high quality jades from previous dynasties. The officers didn't believe him. As far as they were concerned, they looked like the real thing and he was thrown in a holding cell.

The head of Xiamen Museum was called and he came down to assess the jades. After a careful examination he confirmed their suspicions by stating they were authentic. He was taken to see Mr Yao in his cell where he demanded to know where the suspect had acquired these treasures. Had he robbed a tomb? Had he bought them on the black market? Was he part of some smuggling ring?

Mr Yao protested his innocence yet again. He had carved them in his own workshop in Bengbu. He was an expert at making replicas of ancient jades, whether they were from the Hongshan or Liangzhu cultures, the Warring States period, or from the Han, Ming, Qing, Tang or any other Dynasty. He thrust a name card into the museum expert's hand. Look, he told him, it's printed on my name card – occupation, Jade Carver, speciality: *fang gu* or ancient copies. I sell them all over China, he continued. I am just now returning from a business trip.

The expert examined the jades again. This time even more carefully. Cigarettes were offered and a long conversation between the two men ended with the expert offering to buy the two jades from Mr Yao. He had customers in Taiwan who would be very interested in items such as these, he said. Mr Yao's good mood returned. He boarded a later train with more cash in his pocket and an order for some more copies of ancient jades. The expert became a valued and long-term customer.

There is no doubt that the copies that came out of Mr Yao's workshop were very good. He had entered the government factory in Bengbu in 1978 and been given a solid grounding in the making of reproduction jades. Bright and talented, he had branched out on his own after only a few years and further developed the techniques of aging jades to make them look authentic. His work was sought-after all over the country.

Yao Shuming says he never sold his reproductions as the real thing, but knows that some of his customers had no such qualms. He tells of one instance where he sold a customer a copy for US$1,000 and the customer later resold it as an authentic relic for US$70,000. He also confided to me that another customer had been jailed after it was discovered he had sold Mr Yao's work as the real thing.

At that time, Bengbu wasn't famous as a center for reproduction and fake jades. China was still emerging from the shadows and while many in the trade knew of the city's expertise in fashioning high quality copies, the general public was mostly unaware. Money was still very tight in China and there were few people who could afford to buy copies, never mind the real thing. All that most people knew about Bengbu was that it was a violent and lawless place. You took your wallet and your life in your hands if you went there.

This incident highlighted a trade by ruthless merchants who had been buying high quality copies of ancient jades in China for decades and selling them abroad at a huge profit. The main customers of these so-called antique dealers were in places such as Taiwan, Hong Kong, Macao and Singapore. People of Chinese ancestry were an easy target as many of them had a yearning for the ancient traditions of their former homeland.

Dealers also came from North America and Europe where an interest in Chinese antiquities remained strong. Very rarely were the items these dealers bought sold as copies and reproductions. In fact they often came with a certificate of authenticity provided by an expert. Unfortunately many of these experts would issue a certificate without even checking the jade in question – the expert would just count and double check the wad of cash he was given for saying it was a genuine article. Or in some instances, the experts would buy the replicas and then sell them on with certificates of authenticity they issued themselves.

It had all started when a small factory was opened by the government in Bengbu to carve and sell jades for export. While other factories around the country carved in the style of the Ming and Qing, what made the craftsmen of Bengbu different was the skill they had in producing copies from before the Ming Dynasty, founded in 1368. This needed a profound understanding of ancient artifacts and great skill at carving but also a knowledge of the methods used to age a jade in such a way that it looked as though it had emerged discolored and cracked from an ancient tomb.

They had no shortage of customers. Business boomed for the government factory in the 1960s and 1970s, and then in the 1980s and 1990s for craftsmen who set up on their own after the reforms of Deng Xiaoping. But they became victims of their own success. By the late 1990s the export market was saturated. Customers were also becoming aware that they were buying copies rather than the real thing.

Many workshops were saved from closure by a new and even bigger market. Economic reform had put money in the pockets of people on the mainland and they became the main customers. Antique markets and auction houses sprang up all over China for those who had an interest in the country's long and glorious past. Most of the pieces on sale were supplied by workshops in Bengbu that churned out copies by the thousand.

Again, the majority of craftsmen in Bengbu insisted they were making faithful reproductions of jades from ancient dynasties, but the traders who came to buy had no such scruples when it came to selling them. It wasn't long before Bengbu was infamous. There were exposés on national TV and numerous newspaper investigations of its trade in fakes.

One of my early mentors, Huang Hezhong, was very knowledgeable in the field of antique jades and was often consulted by auctioneers and collectors. One day he gave me a book which cataloged the annual sales by the major auction houses in China. He literally cackled with glee as he pointed out fake after fake. In his opinion, eighty percent were modern copies. Other experts have told me this is a conservative estimate. This same book is printed every year and there is no reason to doubt that every year the contents remain just as dubious.

The auction houses are aware of this, but they don't see it as their problem. They do not take responsibility for the authentication of the pieces they sell. This is something the customers must decide for themselves.

Antique emporiums and markets all over the country also have no qualms about trying to pass off copies as the real thing. If you ask the vendors about their jades, they will assure you they are genuine and not copies. They will tell you they have been in their family for generations. They are often laid out sparingly on a cloth on the ground to give the impression their stock is small and each piece is of great value. All of it is fake. There is no way on earth that ancient jades that should be in a museum would be laid out on a black cloth on the ground and offered for sale at knock-down prices. You also have to take into account that every piece on sale and billed as carved before the Ming Dynasty must be either fake or illegal. This is because these ancient jades, if real, are the property of the state.

Fakes are such a big problem that serious Chinese collectors have been going abroad for years to buy because it is much more likely that the pieces that go up for auction outside China have been authenticated. Most of them have provenance. But even this has become a very risky business. The manufacturers of high quality fakes have now started placing their copies in auctions outside China.

Those selling the fakes to people inside and outside China have become ever more ingenious. For some reason, most of them seem to be based in Fujian province. Nowadays they invent a story backed by a photo history for each piece they sell which supposedly documents where each jade came from, which tomb it was dug out of and why it has suddenly come up for sale.

Nowadays many craftsmen in Bengbu plead poverty and tell me they might soon go out of business. They grumble about slow sales because their city is now notorious for producing fakes. They feel hard done-by. They are just hard working carvers, they say, trying to make an honest living producing copies of ancient jades at a modest price.

It may well be true that sales have slowed. It is definitely true that Bengbu is now well known for its fakes and reproductions but there are clear signs that people are still making money. There are five districts in the city where copies are produced and sold. There are more than four thousand workshops and tens of thousands of people making a living in a business that has a turnover of hundreds of millions of dollars a year.

One of the largest districts is known as the Chinese Garden

of Plentiful Jade *zhong hua yu bo yuan*. In this district alone there are more than a thousand workshops where the hum of spindles turning and saws cutting is constant throughout the day.

The district also has a market where hundreds of tons of uncut jade is sold each year. The pieces carved in Bengbu may be fakes, or to be more polite copies, but they are still fashioned from real jade. Unlike other markets in China, most of this is low quality stone which can be bought for as little as US$10 a kilo. Craftsmen in Bengbu don't have to spend lots of money on the material they carve because once they have copied the designs of the ancients, they use various methods to degrade the jade to make it look old, broken and discolored. Nearly all the jade for sale at this market comes from Qinghai province and Siberia. This is not the jade used by ancient neolithic cultures or any of the dynasties that followed. Laboratory tests soon sort out the fakes from the genuine article.

Most craftsmen don't hide the fact they are making copies. The workshops are open to the public and the prices for their pieces are far lower than you would pay for authentic jades. They make no pretense of trying to sell you the real thing. Quite often you can see a dozen Han dynasty dragons of exactly the same design sitting in a display cabinet.

Business may have slowed but the market remains huge. There are more than a hundred cities in China with a population of more than a million and each one has antique shops and perhaps an antique emporium. The National Collectors Association has tens of thousands of members and every province has its own association with hundreds if not thousands of members in each.

Appearances can be deceptive. There may not seem to be much going on in the jade districts of Bengbu but this is a city which now prides itself on being laid-back, where people go to work late, have a long lunch and finish early. (It's a far cry from the wild west atmosphere that ruled here up until the turn of the century). It is also a fact that a great deal of the marketing and selling of the reproductions is done hundreds of miles away in the town of Shenhou in Henan province. So there may not be that many customers in evidence on a daily basis in the workshops of Bengbu, but that doesn't mean the jades carved there aren't being sold somewhere else.

The methods that most workshops use to age the jades are very effective but quite simple. They often bake the pieces in an oven or use a blowtorch to scorch and blacken them. Parts of the stone are often dyed to make it seem weathered and discolored by time and close proximity to other materials. A red dye is used to indicate contamination by cinnabar, which was often used in funeral rites. Cinnabar powder was also sometimes poured into the tomb to deter grave-robbers (it's poisonous) and expel evil spirits. Over the centuries some of this powder sometimes seeped into the stone. Parts of an ancient jade can turn white as the result of exposure to damp and moisture over the centuries, so a white dye is used. And so on and so on.

There is a darker side to all this, though. There are workshops which are far more reticent about what goes on behind closed doors. Everyone in the trade knows where they are, but don't share that information with the public. One of the biggest in Bengbu occupies a three-storey building and houses sixty or seventy workers. On the ground floor are about two dozen carvers. On the first floor a dozen people sit in front of computers in a room which is full of reference books and has the atmosphere of a library. These are the designers who make sure the patterns, whirls and swirls match those on jades excavated from ancient tombs. On the third floor are those who age the jade to make it seem thousands of years old. It is from workshops like these that reproductions end up being sold for tens if not hundreds of thousands of dollars as the real thing. It is to places like these that ruthless merchants from Fujian have been coming for years to buy copies to defraud collectors.

I gained access to this large workshop by posing as a buyer from Europe who was interested in high quality copies of Han Dynasty jades. I showed the owner, photos of the jades I wanted copied (which were in fact from the collection in the British Museum). He just nodded and said no problem - how many copies of each did I want and when did I want them?

None of this is new, of course. There is a rich tradition of producing fakes and copies in China. There is evidence that at least some of the jades in major Western museums are copies rather than the real thing. The Royal Ontario Museum in Canada recently published a book assessing its substantial collection in which the authors raised questions about the authenticity of a few of the exhibits and also pointed out that "During the late Qing Dynasty and the Republic era, there were a number of jade antiquity reproductions that flooded museum collections overseas..."

This doesn't mean that museums around the world were deliberately being sold fakes - at least not most of the time. Authentic jades were so cheap during the buying frenzy of the late 19th and early 20th centuries that there was little reason to manufacture and sell copies, but in the centuries prior to this, many copies were made. Jade carving is such an ancient tradition that there have been collectors in China since well before the birth of Christ. It was not unusual for someone in the Song Dynasty, which ruled China about a thousand years ago, to reproduce a piece from the Han Dynasty more than a thousand years prior to that or for a 19th century carver to recreate a piece from a dynasty in the previous millennium. Through the mists of time, the origin of most of these pieces was forgotten and by the time jades such as these reached Western museums centuries later, they were sometimes mistakenly cataloged.

In 1927 and 1928, Bishop William Charles White, an old China hand acting on behalf of the Royal Ontario Museum, bought twenty-seven objects once owned by the famous nineteenth-century collector and statesman, Wu Dacheng. Some were returned because it was believed they were replicas and according to the authors of the book that reassessed the museum's collection, it is clear that a few are still "problematic in terms of authentication."

Did Wu Dacheng mistakenly catalog the jades he collected? Or was he, a renowned expert, knowingly sold copies? Were they offered to Bishop White in good faith or was he tricked into buying reproductions? We will never know. There is little doubt, though, that a number of jades in museums and private collections in the West may not be what they seem. I leave the reader to make up their own mind. Here is a little tale that might give food for thought.

Early in the twentieth century the department store, Gumps, in San Francisco, started selling jades to the American public. Sales were very good and at one time the store had a Jade Room. Abraham Livingstone Gump even went to China himself to buy stock. His middle man, or Comprador, was named Liu. Early in this friendship A.L. Gump found Liu selling "jade" jewelry manufactured in Germany to visiting tourists.

"It's bad business to cheat your patrons in this way," A.L. commented.

"No matter," Liu philosophized. "One time pigeon, never see again."

"I wouldn't like to have you treat me this way," A.L. persisted.

Liu's face lit up. "Ah no," he exclaimed, "you all time pigeon!"

Those involved in the production of fake antique jades have

been conning people in China for a long time. Westerners have been conned for a much shorter period due to the fact their interest in jade is much more recent.

The manufacture of copies and fakes is not confined to Bengbu. There are other cities in Anhui province where copies are made by the tens of thousands. Tongcheng is renowned for making high-end replicas from the Ming and Qing dynasties. They are particularly famed for making copes of pieces by the legendary Ming Dynasty craftsman, Lu Zigang.

Lu Zigang was Suzhou's greatest jade artisan. The story that is told in jade circles is that his skill was so great that the emperor, Wan Li, summoned him to Beijing to carve in the imperial workshops. Wan Li had been warned that Lu Zigang had the very bad habit of signing his handiwork which was not permitted and most definitely not allowed on pieces made for the imperial household. The emperor was torn between wanting the finest craftsman in the land creating jades for him and suffering a loss of imperial dignity by having those jades signed by a common artisan.

He decided to test Lu Zigang by having him carve a teapot out of a piece of mutton-fat-white jade. He ordered him, on pain of death, not to sign it. The craftsman duly carved the teapot and presented it to the monarch. It was a beautiful piece and confirmed in the eyes of the emperor that Lu Zigang was indeed a craftsman without equal. But it was only after Wan Li had examined it in minute detail and was sure that the artisan had not signed it that he broke into a smile, showered him with gold and allowed him to leave.

The emperor was so enamored of the teapot that he kept it close and would often pick it up to admire the superb craftsmanship. He would turn it over and over in his hands and enjoy its beauty. On one sunny day he was doing just this when a shaft of sunlight shone on the jade. Peering closely, Wan Li could just make out the name, Lu Zigang, etched very faintly inside the spout.

What happened after this varies depending on who tells the story. Some say Wan Li smashed the teapot in a fury and ordered the carver put to death. Others say that in spite of being tricked he was so in love with his work that he forgave Lu Zigang and allowed him to live and continue to practice his craft. Whatever the truth of it some of Lu Zigang's jades still exist and can be seen in museums in Beijing, Taipei and Shanghai. He is the only jade carver from imperial times who is remembered. No others ever signed their work and their names have been lost forever.

I am also reliably informed that at least one piece by Lu Zigang on display in a Western museum is a copy. It's not a modern copy but was one of many done in tribute to his work by craftsmen in the later Qing Dynasty. When I asked the expert who told me this how he knew this just from the photo I showed him he reeled off a list of reasons including the dimensions of the piece and the inferior quality of the jade used. This Qing Dynasty copy is valuable in itself. At auction it would sell for about US$50,000. The original, though, would fetch half a million. I have had a modern copy made of the same piece. It cost me US$500.

It is not beyond the realms of possibility that some very skilled craftsman has created a new piece in the style of this long-dead master which has been sold on by an unscrupulous merchant to a multi-millionaire. It might well be that this rich collector is convinced that he has a previously undiscovered masterpiece by Lu Zigang sitting in his collection. He would be wrong.

It must also be remembered that the current generation of master carvers in China cut their teeth making copies of jades from previous dynasties. It is only in this century that they have begun to dip their toes in the waters of original design. It is still quite common for a master carver to fashion jades in the style of a particular dynasty.

I know of one craftsman in Suzhou who makes exquisite copies of Ming and Qing Dynasty pieces. His customers come to him with pictures of the originals and ask him to copy them. He complies. In his eyes, he is not making fakes, he is making copies to order for people who cannot afford the original jades. What the customers do with them is none of his concern. He is a very rich man. When I first met him, I always wondered why his workshop was out of the public eye in a run-down building and he didn't have a shop displaying his jades. Once I learned of his speciality, I stopped wondering why.

The majority of Chinese buyers know most of what is for sale are copies, fakes, whatever you want to call them. I like to think of them as modern reproductions in the same way you can buy modern reproduction furniture in the West. My mother bought a beautiful medieval knight's chest in polished oak which I still have. It is made from oak like the original. It is the same design. It looks beautiful. My mother treasured it and I love it but I am under no illusions that it is the real thing. It wasn't cheap but it was a fraction of the price I would have had to pay for the original and to my eyes looks just as good if not better.

Most Chinese people don't have the funds to buy the real thing but they want to own something which represents an ancient part of their culture and history. The fakes are very good and would not look out of place in a tastefully furnished apartment in any city in China. A good analogy would be high class prints of oil paintings by the great European masters like Rembrandt, Leonardo da Vinci or Tintoretto which grace the walls of the homes of art lovers in the West. Those who buy and display them know they are not real but it doesn't lessen their enjoyment of them.

A final thought. If you visit a museum in China and take some enjoyment from viewing their jades, do not be surprised to learn that many of them are fakes. Museums in cities across China often buy them to put on display. They do this for three reasons. The first is because they don't always have the real thing. The second is for security - if they do have the originals, they don't want to risk them being stolen. The third is in order not to damage the originals through constant exposure to light. Nothing in China and especially in the world of jade is quite what it seems.

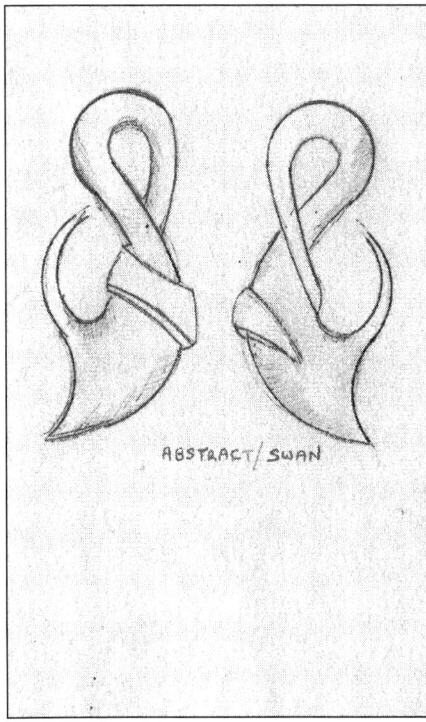

13

MULTI-MILLIONAIRE COLLECTORS

LI YUAN is a petite woman with close-cropped black hair who is in the habit of wearing flowing, ankle length cotton robes in deep colors. She is a bundle of energy and looks on everything with shrewd eyes which sparkle with energy and humor. She is not young but neither does she appear old. As with many

Asian women, it is difficult to determine her age. Li Yuan has a warm smile and is very charming, but there is steel beneath the surface. It is perhaps the only way a woman could have become so successful in business in such a male-dominated culture.

I have no idea of her true worth or standing in Chinese society but she has a list of contacts that go all the way to the top and even reach back into history. She is not only friends with the great and the good of modern China but also with its ancient royalty. One of the rooms in her very spacious home is decorated with photos of her with the descendants of the last emperor and empress of China.

She is called Jade Sister by her close friends, because of her fascination with jade. She has a fabulous collection with pieces ancient and modern. Some of her favorite pieces are thousands of years old and date back to the prehistoric Hongshan and Liangzhu cultures.

Many of them can be seen on display in cabinets in a special room she has set aside for them in her house in a quiet and prosperous village in the Tongzhou district on the outskirts of Beijing. It is a large house. It has to be to accommodate herself and the five servants who cater to her every need.

She has a personal doctor on hand twenty-four hours a day to guard her health, a married couple who act as cook and gardener, a chauffeur and, of course, a bodyguard to protect her from kidnappers. She is an extremely rich woman and is right to be cautious about security not only for herself but also for her fabulous collection of jades. The room they are displayed in is larger than most houses in the village.

Her staff may be servants but they seem more like a family. Meals are taken together. It is one of the few times you might bump into her bodyguard. He is very discreet. When her friends visit, he makes himself scarce. It is only when those who are less well-known come calling, perhaps on business, that he becomes a quiet presence by her side.

Apart from the jade room in her house there is also an entire building nearby for her collection of hand-stitched Beijing Opera costumes. She has the biggest private collection in China. Li Yuan made her first appearance in the national opera at the age of twelve and has never lost her passion for singing. Her parents were both performers and she was trained in the traditional style from the age of six or seven.

If China had not opened up to the West she might well have made the national opera her life. As a young woman this seemed to be her destiny. She married one of the opera musicians and they had a son. It was only then that she realized that if they were to give their child a good start in life they would need to earn more than the starvation wages paid by the Beijing Opera. Her monthly salary in 1984 was the equivalent of US$6. Her husband earned even less.

So she went into business and began to make a lot of money. Her son remembers her regularly coming home in the 1980s with carrier bags full of cash. He has memories of it being counted on the kitchen table. The amounts varied but were usually about US$20,000. A fortune at the time.

One of her first business ventures was selling medical equipment manufactured by a factory in Inner Mongolia. On her frequent trips to the factory, she couldn't help but notice a beautiful stone figurine on the desk in the manager's office. She told him how much she admired it and he gave it to her as a gift. He also told her that he had another piece like it at home which she could have.

Li Yuan couldn't explain why she loved the pieces that the manager gave to her. They were obviously very old and even though eroded and discolored by time, they had a dignity and mystery about them that spoke to her soul. From then on, every time she went to the factory she would visit the surrounding villages and buy old stone carvings from local people. She sometimes paid less than a dollar per piece.

This was the start of her collection. They were jades from the prehistoric Hongshan culture. They weren't worth very much at the time. They were highly prized by archaeologists, but the craze for collecting ancient jades had not yet begun and prices were low. It wasn't until the start of the twenty-first century that their true value became apparent. That first piece given to her by the factory manager is now valued at hundreds of thousands of dollars.

Li Yuan didn't buy her jades to make money. She bought them because she loved them. Nearly all the pieces she bought at first were nephrite jades carved by ancient cultures. She was too busy investing in a dozen business ventures to worry about making a profit from them. Medical equipment from Inner Mongolia, exporting sheepskins from Hebei, opening restaurants, hotels and a myriad of other money-making schemes occupied her time.

Financial success also brought personal heartbreak. China is a very traditional society and her husband could not accept his wife being the main breadwinner. They divorced. This is a common story in modern China. There are very few men who will play second fiddle to a woman. Things are changing rapidly but this ancient poem still sums up the attitude of many people in China today:

> "When a son is born,
> Let him sleep in a bed.
> Clothe him with fine dress and and give him jades
> to play with.

How Lordly is his cry,
May he grow up to wear crimson
And be lord of the clan and tribe.

When a daughter is born,
Let her sleep on the ground.
Wrap her in common cloth,
And give her broken tiles to play with.
May she have no faults or virtues of her own,
May she well attend to food and wine,
And bring no discredit to her parents."

This was written more than a thousand years ago. It reflects a way of thinking that goes back even further than that and while China is moving forward, it is difficult to change a mindset which has existed for so long.

Li Yuan never remarried and her energies focused on business and her passion for nephrite. She never fell in love with the sister stone, jadeite. It didn't sing to her soul in the same way. But perhaps, ironically, she did make a lot of money from selling jadeite. Her younger brother was the general in charge of the army in Yunnan, the province bordering Myanmar where jadeite is mined. The army often confiscated boulders from traders trying to smuggle them into the country to avoid paying import tax. She was able to buy this confiscated stone at a bargain price, send it to factories to have it carved into pendants, figurines and bangles and then sell them for a huge profit. Ever the shrewd businesswoman, she got out of the jadeite trade in 2014 just before a market slump.

Her passion for ancient jades continued to grow. She was a frequent visitor to the now legendary Ghost Market in Beijing which was held in the 1980s and 1990s between midnight and four in the morning. This market was operated in the dark and customers had to bring a torch to examine the goods on sale. There were strict rules. The main one was you could shine a torch on the jades but could not shine it to show the face of the vendor. Anonymity was very important as many of them had robbed graves to obtain the artifacts that were now becoming so sought after by the newly rich.

Li Yuan's collection grew and grew. By the turn of the century, the Ghost Market began to fade out of existence as controls on the sale of cultural relics became more stringent. Nature (and business) abhor a vacuum, however, and a market called *pan jia yuan* started up selling so-called cultural relics. Over the years, it has become a thriving tourist attraction with thousands of stalls selling bric-a-brac. Finding a genuine ancient jade on sale at this market would be like finding the fabled Unicorn's Egg. There is a misconception that if you get to *pan jia yuan* very early in the morning, there are some bona fide ancient jades on sale. Perhaps this rumor came about because people had heard about the Ghost Market and were under the impression it still existed in some form. It doesn't.

Li Yuan is semi-retired now. She has sold some of her businesses and leaves the running of most of the others to family members and trusted aides. She is still a bundle of energy and concentrates on her two passions, jade and opera. She has hundreds of opera students across China who she teaches both online and in person. Discussions are under way with the Beijing authorities to house her fabulous collection of opera costumes in a specially built museum. And she still buys jade when the fancy takes her. Unlike most people who have either the soul of an artist or a head for business both these talents seem to live in harmony inside her.

Very early in her collecting days, she realized the value of the small jade beads that were found in most tombs. Grave robbers would ask high prices for the larger pieces like the *huangs* and *bi* discs they found but would sell the beads by the bag. Jade Sister snapped them up and now owns thousands of them. She creates beautiful necklaces and bracelets from them which she sells for fabulous prices to the rich and famous or donates to auctions which raise money for good causes. She also gives them away to her many friends.

When Jade Sister started collecting, very few others were doing the same thing. There are now tens of thousands of serious collectors across China. There are the super rich who collect jades both ancient and modern and never seem to worry about the price. There are many more from the middle classes with more modest pocketbooks. Scratch the surface of China and a love of jade is found everywhere.

There are those who both love jade and also see it as a financial investment. Richard Pang is one of these people. He and his business partners invest in jade both ancient and modern. Like most of those with a serious interest in jade and Chinese culture he is a modest man of refinement and taste. He is not one of the brash new rich who flaunt their wealth and are known as "*you qian mei you wen hua*" which literally translates as "have money have no culture."

Mr Pang dresses well but not ostentatiously. He doesn't wear designer labels, just a good quality suit and tie with hand- made leather shoes. What makes him stand out is his jewelry. The first time I saw him, he was wearing a bracelet made of eight carved pebbles of the best Hetian mutton-fat-white jade. It was a beautiful piece of work with the luster of old jade. Each pebble was carved differently. The stones had that slight oily sheen that is possessed by only the very best white jade. A Western man wearing such a bracelet might seem a little odd, but it looked just right on Mr Pang.

I met him through my addiction to coffee. Every morning at eight o'clock, on my way to Chinese classes at Suzhou University I would make a detour to the only Starbucks in the old town. In those days (2009), he and a woman I later learned was his wife were the only customers apart from myself at that time of day. Starbucks hadn't caught on yet. Nowadays, you can't move for Chinese people sipping their cappuccinos. At first we were just on nodding terms. But I was fascinated by his bracelet. One day I couldn't resist. I walked up to him and his wife and said in my very bad Chinese.

"That's a beautiful bracelet you have."

He smiled politely and glanced down at it. "Thank you. It is nothing really. Just a cheap piece I wear for sentimental reasons."

It is good manners in China to be modest. And he was being very modest about something that was probably worth a small fortune. He held out his wrist so that I could examine it more closely.

"It's made of jade," he said.

Chinese people always say this as though they think Westerners have no idea what jade is. This used to irritate me until I realized that virtually all Westerners have no idea what jade is.

We fell into conversation as his wife looked on and sipped her coffee. A friendship had begun. We started to chat every morning about jade and the world in general. One day I walked into the coffee shop and Richard sprang from his seat.

"I have something to show you."

He produced two small, intricately carved wooden boxes, and carefully laid them on the table in front of me.

"Go on," he said. "Open them."

I sat down and picked up one of the boxes. I took off the lid and inside was a jade pendant. It was off-white in color. The carving was quite simple but it was a beautiful piece. It felt smooth and slightly oily to the touch. It wasn't the highest quality jade, but I had an inkling it was a very old and valuable piece. It was a thin oblong of white jade. The carving on it was minimal but beautifully done. The stone itself was good but not outstanding. I wore a piece myself which was probably higher quality stone. I looked at it for a long time before handing it back and reaching for the other one.

Richard often had a piece of jade to show me when I arrived at the coffee shop. After a while I began to notice that on these occasions his wife became anxious and sometimes glanced nervously at the door. She seemed uncomfortable with her husband pulling jades worth tens of thousands of dollars out of a plastic bag in a public place. Perhaps she was afraid that masked men would come and rob her husband of these treasures. It never happened, but the objects he pulled out of carrier bags on a regular basis were a joy to behold.

At first I was a little suspicious about why he was showing me these exquisite pieces. More than once, I had been befriended by someone who then tried to sell me very poor jades at exorbitant prices while swearing blind to their superb quality. But this was different. Richard had no intention of trying to sell me anything. He just wanted to share his passion for a stone which enchanted him as much as it did me.

One day, he showed me an especially beautiful piece which I drooled over for long enough to be late for class (again). He then mentioned it was one of the smaller pieces in his collection and perhaps, if I had time, I would like to come to his shop to see some more. This was the first I had heard about a collection, so I said I would be delighted. We arranged a day and time and before I could ask directions on how to get there he told me he would come to pick me up.

On the appointed day, he appeared at my door and I was whisked off to a very large shop with high ceilings, white walls and very few goods on display. It was near to Suzhou Museum but a little off the tourist trail. There were no customers. Richard said I should make myself comfortable and then disappeared upstairs. The manager of the shop came over and introduced himself, offered me tea and then left me to my own devices. What followed was one of the most pleasant afternoons I have had in a long and eventful life.

After a few minutes, Richard bustled in and we went upstairs to an office and sat down at a large, highly polished table. Richard fired off some rapid Chinese to the manager who nodded and promptly disappeared. When he came back a few minutes later, he was carrying an object covered with a dark velvet cloth which he placed very carefully in the center of the table. With great ceremony, he slowly removed the cloth to reveal a beautiful piece of pure white jade.

It was about eighteen inches high and carved into the shape of a stylized mountain. On it were three figures in a cave. There were trees, animals and birds cut into the jade. It was one of the most beautiful pieces I had ever seen. I have a memory of gaping open-mouthed at it. I went to touch it. I wanted to feel the stone in my hands. I hesitated and looked at Richard. He nodded.

It was exquisite. I turned it round in my hands and savored its beauty. That was just the first piece. Next came two immaculately smooth snuff bottles, perfectly rounded and beautiful in their simplicity from the time of the Emperor Qianlong, in the late eighteenth century. While I had less interest in old jades, these were beautiful to look at and touch. More jades followed. There was a piece that Richard had bought by telephone auction from Tokyo. (Many great pieces of jade had been pillaged by the Japanese during the War and were now being reclaimed at great cost by collectors in China) and a bowl from the late Tang Dynasty, more than a thousand years old. After what seemed like only a few minutes, Richard said, "Andrew, we have to go now. The time lock on the vault only gives a limited amount of time and we need to put the jades back."

I could swear I had only been sitting at that table a few minutes when he spoke but two hours had passed. In all, I had looked at, handled and asked questions about seven pieces, both ancient and modern. My face must have looked a picture. Richard laughed. He then dumbfounded me further by telling me that next time we could have a look at the really good stuff.

I have no idea how rich my friend is, but he is one of the partners who owns the luxury mall that the Starbucks was housed in. I think he may have owned the coffee shop as well. It didn't actually open until eight thirty and he liked a quiet half hour with his wife before going to his office and getting on with the business of the day. He was just far too polite to tell me I was gatecrashing his early morning quiet time.

There are many people like Richard Pang and Jade Sister dotted around China. They are cultured, and intelligent people who are passionate about jade and steeped in Chinese culture. You would not notice them in the street and Westerners very rarely come into contact with them. They do not seek out foreigners. If you are lucky enough to meet them and have the time to get to know them, they can give you a window into the real China.

There is a common misconception in the West that only antique and ancient jades are sold at auction. The fact is, in China, many jade auctions are of contemporary pieces. As mentioned earlier nearly all of the ancient jades that go up for auction are fakes and many collectors in China do not bother with them.

Jades by modern masters, on the other hand, often fetch higher prices. In many people's eyes (including my own), the carving is far superior and the jade used of much higher quality.

One of the most prestigious auction houses in Beijing only deals in works by the modern masters. It holds between four and six auctions a year and produces four catalogs for each. The first catalog is for jades with a reserve price of up to US$8,000, the second for jades with a reserve price of up to US$15,000, the third with a reserve price of up to a US$100,000 and the fourth catalog is for people who do not have to ask the price. The highest price achieved by a modern master for a single jade by this auction house was just under US$2 million. That was for nephrite jade. Modern jadeite carvings command even more money.

There is another type of auction which appears to be uniquely Chinese. People make bids until the reserve price is reached then no more bids are made. I have attended auctions like these in three Chinese cities and the format might differ slightly, but the reserve price is never exceeded.

They are reasonably quiet affairs often organized by a city's jade association. The pieces on offer are not usually the work of nationally recognized master carvers but younger craftsmen and those who have achieved the status of provincial master. Quite often the auction is preceded by a question and answer session where a panel of craftsmen answer questions about all things related to jade. Then bids are made for jades carved by those on the panel. These pieces always seem to sell. This may be because friends of those on the panel sitting in the audience will pretend to buy the piece if the reserve price is not reached. A carver would lose too much face if a piece failed to sell while he was sitting there watching the bidding. The prices achieved at these affairs are usually only a few hundred dollars. Sometimes a piece will go for between one and two thousand.

Online auctions are increasingly popular. I know the owner of one large workshop who recently started doing such auctions. At the first, he sold sixty jade necklaces in thirty seconds. Admittedly this is not an avenue open to every carver. My friend has a well-known and trusted brand and a very large stock. His future is looking very rosy.

In the meantime, traditional auction houses continue to do good business but in new ways. Gone are the heady days when rich customers with numbered placards would pack an auction room and bid against each other for a prized jade. The events are now quieter with fewer customers. After all, why travel all the way to an auction house if you can see something online, pay for it using a mobile phone app and have it delivered by courier.

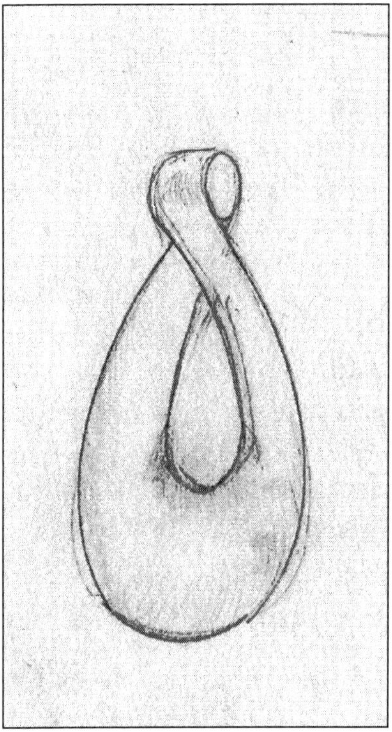

14

Advice on Buying Jade

Before giving advice on choosing and purchasing jade, it is important to stress that the consumer culture in China is very different from that in the West. One of the first things I bought when I arrived was an electric kettle. I went to a shop and selected the kettle I wanted. It was in a sealed box. I took the box to the counter and handed it to the sales assistant and reached into my wallet to pay for it. Instead of taking my money she unsealed and opened the box to show me there was a kettle inside. She then took it out, filled it with water and plugged it in to show me that it actually worked. Only then did she accept my money.

When it comes to any sort of consumer goods China is what you might call a "low trust" society. Scandals about fake and faulty consumer products, tainted medicine and adulterated foodstuffs are common. Chinese people are much more cautious when buying something than people in the West. They are well aware that a lot of what is on sale is, to say the least, substandard.

Foreigners need to be especially cautious. They are treated differently from Chinese people when it comes to shopping. I once bought a computer at a reputable chain store only to find out when I got it home that it was faulty. (I had not insisted on the box being opened to see if the computer worked properly). I immediately took it back to the shop and approached the sales assistant who had sold it to me to get my money back. After two hours of patient conversation he refused to refund my money and suggested I contact the manufacturer. This was in spite of the fact that there was a very large sign on the wall of the store which stated in Chinese and English that if, within seven days, customers were unhappy with their purchase for any reason they could get a refund with no questions asked. I even walked him over to the sign and read it out to him in both languages. No dice. As far as he was concerned I should have checked the computer worked before I left the store. I then phoned my wife and let her speak to the assistant. She got me a refund after speaking to him for only thirty seconds.

So when it comes to buying jade, Westerners have to be very, very, very careful. Foreigners are generally seen as easy marks who don't know the value of what they are buying, don't haggle and pay way too much. In my first years as a jade carver, I used to sell my work in a weekend market at a Confucian temple in the center of old Suzhou. It was a local market which rarely saw anyone from the West. When the odd, intrepid explorer did walk in, a ripple of excitement would spread through the market and the mood changed to one of expectation. Smiles broadened and prices went up. I am not ashamed to say my prices doubled.

I don't sell at that market any more. Nowadays I exhibit and sell at my teahouse and jade gallery. I often give talks on jade to groups of foreigners who are interested in Chinese culture. These talks are very popular. Guests are served finger sandwiches, fresh baked scones with organic jam and clotted cream and a selection of cakes in the ground floor tearoom overlooking Jinji Lake while I prattle on about all things jade. As they sip their tea and butter their scones, they are free to ask questions and show me jades they have bought. I am sorry to say that quite often my assessment can ruin a guest's appetite.

Almost without exception they have paid far too much. Quite often what they have bought is not even jade. Here is an example. An elderly American couple produced a silver ring with a very small green stone which they had bought the previous week at a tourist spot in Beijing for US$1,200. The ring was worth US$15 at most. The conversation they had with the merchant had gone something like this:

Elderly American couple: "Is this jade?"

Merchant: "Yes, yes, very good jade."

Elderly American couple: "How much is it?"

Merchant: "Twelve hundred."

Elderly American couple: "Is that twelve hundred dollars?"

Merchant: (after a slight hesitation) "Yes."

The merchant most definitely meant twelve hundred Chinese

RMB which works out at under two hundred dollars. If the elderly American couple had been prepared to haggle he would have come down to maybe a hundred dollars which was still five or six times what the ring was worth. They told me they didn't even haggle.

I have no idea what type of small stone was set in the ring they bought but it definitely wasn't jade. There are so many lookalikes and imitations that it is difficult to tell which one it was. It could have been quartz, agate, bowenite, serpentine, jasper, marble, maw sit sit, chalcedony or any one of a dozen other stones. I have seen colored glass and even plastic sold at tourist markets as jade.

In my early days, I was also a victim of unscrupulous merchants. I often paid too much for the stone I bought. I would moan about this to my wife. She would look at me in exasperation and say, "If you don't know, don't buy!" It was the same with my first teacher, Wufan; he would laugh uproariously at the fact that I had been conned yet again. It's very much "sold as seen" in China. You have to be clear you know what you are doing when you buy jade, or anything else for that matter.

With all this in mind, where you choose to make your purchase is very important. You should be very sure that the merchant in question has a good reputation and sells genuine jade. Shops in tourist areas are to be avoided at all costs, especially by foreigners. The same goes for tourist markets. At the end of the day, the vendors know you won't be coming back for a refund so they have no qualms in trying to sell you overpriced imitations. As with tourist shops all over the world, you will be sold cheap rubbish at an exorbitant mark up by merchants who are delighted to relieve you of your money.

High-end shopping malls in cities throughout China all have jades for sale. The jade on offer is usually genuine. For those who are uncomfortable with the idea of haggling and like to see each piece with a price tag on it, these are good places to browse. Quite often they are clustered together with shops selling gold and diamond jewelry. Nephrite and jadeite are always displayed separately so you can be sure of which type of stone you are buying.

This is a safe way of buying reasonable quality jade in a comfortable air-conditioned environment but there are a number of reasons why I would make it a last resort. The first is that the stores are usually part of a chain which has hundreds of outlets across China. They buy in bulk and the jade is never of the highest quality. A jade Buddha purchased in Beijing will be exactly the same as one purchased at one of their other stores in Shanghai, Xi'an or any number of other cities. They are production-line pieces, often pre-formed by computer and only finished by hand rather than the work of a skilled craftsman.

The labelling and any information given by the sales assistant can also be misleading. You will be told it is carved from the famous Hetian jade. It might seem a bargain at a few hundred dollars but further questioning would reveal it is the common-or-garden mountain jade, not the sought-after seed jade plucked from the White Jade River.

It might look beautiful under the display lighting, but you need to take it out of the case and see it in natural daylight to assess its true color and translucency. No sales assistant is going to allow you to take it out of the mall to do this. Go to a jade shop, however, and most of them will have no problem with you carrying a piece out into the street to examine it.

While shopping malls offer items with prices clearly labeled, the price is still negotiable. The sales assistants have clear instructions on how big a discount they can give. In my experience, this is usually up to fifty percent. So if you see a jade you like priced at US$500 and your budget is US$300, then you are in with a fighting chance. Quite often, your offer will be refused by the sales assistant, but if you walk away it is not uncommon for them to seek you out before you leave the store and either agree to sell at the price you suggested or at least make a reasonable counter-offer.

Jade is also on sale in the duty free zones of international airport terminals. This is where businessmen who have been too busy to buy presents for loved ones back home buy last-minute gifts. The prices are outrageous and while there are a few outlets that sell the genuine article, if you are in a hurry, you well may end up buying rubbish at an exorbitant price.

A much better bet than a shopping mall is a jade mall or a street of shops where all that is sold is jade. They can be found in major cities all over China and you can almost guarantee that what is on sale is high quality. They are usually air-conditioned, very tastefully laid out and great places to spend an afternoon window shopping. Unfortunately there are no price tags and haggling is essential. Prices also tend to be high.

If you are lucky enough to be in a city with a jade carving district, then it is a much better idea to seek out the workshops that supply the jade malls and shops. They will be very glad of your business and you should be able to negotiate far better prices. Target the tiny workshops with just one craftsman. They are usually run by young carvers just starting out who are strapped for cash and hungry for sales. Sometimes a sweet little piece can be picked up for a couple of hundred dollars. If it costs less, then walk away. No half-decent piece of jade, however small, is going to cost less than that.

A note here on bangles. They are extremely popular with women in China because they symbolize harmony and eternity. There is also a belief that they can protect the wearer from harm.

It is commonly believed, for example, that if a person is in a car crash then the bangle will break instead of the wearer's limbs. They can also be a status symbol. Very high quality jade bangles are often worn by successful businesswomen. A lot of the most successful people dress quite casually and do not stand out from the common herd, but an expensive bangle gives off a subtle signal that this is someone who has made it in the world and should be taken seriously.

Never go to a shopping mall if you want to buy a bangle. Have it custom-made to fit your wrist. Seek out a craftsman who will make one for you. Choose the stone yourself and haggle. Never forget to haggle.

People who buy bangles off-the-shelf will often end up disappointed. It might be a couple of years before they realize they have been cheated. Bangles are mass-produced in Pingzhou in Guangdong and Shifosi in Henan. They make them in bulk to cut costs with what can only be described as brutal industrial processes (brutal to the jade that is). As a result, quite a few end up with hairline cracks and flaws. These are not discarded. Tried and tested methods are used to hide the cracks and make them saleable. With nephrite bangles they inject hot wax into the stone under high pressure. This fills the small cracks in the stone and makes them appear flawless - at least for a while. Then the jade begins to look worn and tired and the cracks reappear. By then it is far too late to go back to the store and ask for a refund.

Jadeite bangle manufacturers use a different technique. They cut slabs of poor quality stone and bleach them in a bath of strong acid for a few weeks then inject colored resin into the stone before carving it into bangles. Yet again the color starts to fade after a few years.

For the bangle I carved my wife as a betrothal gift, I selected the stone myself. I spent a week getting it just right. It replaced the jadeite bangle she had been wearing when I first met her. It was the second thing I noticed about her (after how beautiful she was). That jadeite bangle had been treated and the color was already beginning to fade. It is not just Westerners who are vulnerable. Chinese merchants will take advantage of anyone they can.

Choose the right craftsman and the right stone, however, and you will have a beautiful piece of jewelry that will last you the rest of your life. Good jade is harder and harder to find and a high-quality bangle will only increase in value. It can also be handed down from generation to generation.

A very important personal item is the so-called jade "chop" or "seal." While in the West people will sign a contract, in China they use what is called a chop or seal to do the same thing. A Chinese character or series of characters is carved into the bottom of a piece of stone which is dipped in red ink and stamped on official documents. No business in China can run without a set of company chops or seals. Possession of them is treated very seriously and when not in use they are usually locked away in a safe. While carving them is considered a traditional craft they are also an essential part of modern business. Chinese companies can use an electronic chop in the same way that we in the West use an electronic signature.

Nowadays, a company or personal chop is sometimes not considered adequate and has to be accompanied by a handwritten signature as a more secure form of identification. I learned this when the Suzhou Jade Association sent out letters to foreign artists inviting them to participate in an exhibition. Each letter was "chopped" with the official seal of the association but they were rejected by the visa sections of Chinese embassies throughout the world because the Association head had not added his handwritten signature. No visas were granted until new letters were prepared with both a chop and a signature.

There are many places where you can get a personalized chop made up while you wait but do not be fooled into thinking it is jade they use. Jade is so hard it would take a skilled craftsman at least a day to carve such a chop. They usually use sandstone. I made one in jade for my wife and it took me two days to carve four characters into the seal.

I was hoping that she would use it for business. It came in an elegant satin-lined case and I thought it looked rather smart. It is still sitting on the shelf at home unused. Nearly everyone seems to use rubber stamps and red ink instead nowadays. Even the officials in the Arts and Crafts Museum, who are the guardians of Chinese culture, use rubber stamps.

I do occasionally make chops to order for customers but it is usually a vanity project rather than something to be used for official purposes. They often end up as expensive paperweights.

Wherever you go to buy jade, even if it is to a reputable store or craftsman, it is good to have an idea of how to identify good from bad and real from fake. There are some basic indicators you can use to do this. The first is the scratch test. Both jadeite and nephrite are harder than steel so you should not be able to scratch them with a penknife. This is not a foolproof test and if you try it in a shopping mall they might well call security and have you thrown out of the building.

Another test is what I call the "Heft Test." Just toss the jade into the air and feel the weight of it. Jade is very dense and weighs more than other stones. You can do a comparison with an ordinary pebble picked up in the street to feel the difference. Again, it's not an ideal test as it cannot be used if the jade is set with gold and other precious stones which change the "heft."

Another indicator is what I call the "Warmth Test." Hold a piece of jade in your hand until it reaches body temperature, then place it on the table for thirty seconds. When you pick it up, it should be cold again. If it isn't, it might well be glass.

A useful tool when assessing jade is a very good torch. Shining a powerful torch into a jade will reveal slight imperfections in the stone. This is a good thing for two reasons. The first is that it shows it is probably a genuine stone. Man-made material tends to be very even in texture. Glass for example is uniform in texture. A lot of cheaper imitation jades are made of colored and treated glass. The second reason is that pointing out slight imperfections is a good bargaining move. Any form of mottling, dark irregular specks, or blemishes reduces the value.

If you can, wait for an overcast day to buy jade. Never buy a jade on a sunny day. It always looks good in the sunshine. It's almost as deceptive as good display lighting. Examine jade on a dull overcast day in natural light. This will give you a better idea of its quality.

You can do all these tests while chatting to the merchant or craftsman. He will have a very good idea of what you are doing. These are all things that he might do himself if he was buying jade. Do not even consider asking the price until after you have done them. Just doing these tests might bring the price down. If you are in a jade mall or street of shops, try visiting a few to practice your technique and also to get an idea of prices. A merchant at one shop might be honest and ask a reasonable amount while the merchant next door, on seeing a foreigner enter, might just see dollar signs and rack up his prices.

Generally speaking the same advice holds when you are buying both nephrite and jadeite. The most important things are color, texture and translucency. The more saturated it is with a good color, the better.

The colors that are most prized in jadeite are the greens and purples. My favorite is the type of purple which looks to me like a soft lavender. For nephrite, the favored colors are white, green, yellow, black and porcelain. Porcelain jade is white and black jade layered together in the same stone. Sometimes the layers are quite distinct. Sometimes they blend together in parts of the stone to add a subtle grey to the white and black. This makes possible some remarkably ingenious use of color in carving.

If you have decided you are going to buy jade, then first set your budget and go searching for a piece that speaks to your heart. Either buy a carving you like or buy a piece of jade jewelry. Why do I suggest jade jewelry? Because insurance companies in the West generally don't understand modern jade. The jade amulet I wear every day was carved from a pebble that was bought for cash at a jade market. Today it is probably worth about US$5,000 but I have no proof of purchase, and even if I took it to an expert for valuation there is no certainty that they would know its worth. Experts in the Western world know about antique jades, but not about modern pieces. If I took it back to England it would be very difficult to insure.

On the other hand, jewelry which combines jade with gold and other precious stones is something insurance companies do understand. Some of my best pieces have been jade combined with gold, rubies, sapphires and diamonds. And forget about this nine-carat gold nonsense - it hardly counts as gold. All jewelry, in my opinion, should be made with eighteen-carat gold. Good enough to glow and hard enough to last.

A good rule of thumb for jade jewelry is this. Good jade warrants eighteen-carat gold, real diamonds, sapphires and rubies. So if you see a piece combined with silver, zirconia and semi-precious stones it should cost far less.

Good jade is expensive. Think of it this way, you wouldn't go to a flea market to buy a diamond engagement ring. If a stall holder showed you what he claimed to be a diamond ring, you would be very suspicious. It is the same with jade, which in China is considered a precious stone. Buy jade from a market stall in China and you can bet your bottom dollar it will be poor quality, if it is jade at all. You need to go into a jade shop or a high-end mall to get the real thing.

I don't sell cheap jades. Neither does any decent jade shop in China. There is a saying in China which is the same in the West - *yi fen jia qian yi fen huo*, which roughly translates as you get what you pay for.

Haggling is a way of life in China. It is part of the culture and a process usually enjoyed by all those who enter into any sort of agreement. The initial asking price is just the beginning of a negotiation. Most people in the jade business are very traditional and are often astounded that foreigners don't haggle. I belong to a few jade-carving forums and chat groups where photos are often posted of a smiling craftsman together with a Western customer holding the jade they have just purchased. These photos usually have a note attached something along the lines of "He paid $$$$ and didn't even haggle!!"

There is an art to haggling. Many Westerners feel uncomfortable with the process because it appears confrontational. This could not be further from the truth. China is a non-confrontational society. Unlike most people in the West, Chinese people will go all around the houses before coming to the point and saying what they mean. So don't think of haggling in this way. When watched from the outside there may seem to be a lot shouting, gesticulation, disgusted expressions and indignation on both sides, but it is just part of a game. The buyer and seller both have a price in mind. If agreement can be reached, there will suddenly be smiles all round. It is not a process designed to upset people, just a way of reaching agreement by both sides without losing face.

What you should not do is haggle, agree a price and then walk away without buying. This is extremely bad manners. Just enjoy the process. Don't rush it. If you have time, spend an afternoon examining jades and asking questions. There is a reason jade has been treasured by so many cultures all over the world across the centuries. Jade, whether it is nephrite or jadeite, is a very special stone. At some point you will come across a piece that speaks to your heart and soul.

Which brings me to a final note for serious collectors who might want to splash out thousands or tens of thousands of dollars on a jade. You could try an auction of modern jades but perhaps a better way is to go to one of the renowned master carvers directly. Choose the carver carefully, make sure he is actually an officially recognized master carver. There are many craftsmen who will tell foreigners they are master carvers but they might not be telling the whole story. The title of master carver is given at local, provincial and national level. The only title worth having is that awarded at national level.

The stamp of a famous national master carver on a jade increases the value dramatically. Their pieces often fetch more than those of ancient jades that come up for auction, but check the stamp carefully. There will be one for a piece done by the master himself and another stamp for a piece designed by him but carved by one of the craftsmen in his workshop. Both have great value, but the piece by the master will be more expensive and much more collectable.

There are about two hundred master carvers in China but not all of them are working. Some have the title but have retired. Even among those with the title there are those who stand out. For example there are fifteen masters in Suzhou but four of them are acknowledged as head and shoulders above the rest.

You will also get a better price if you are prepared to go to the workshop of a master and sit down and have tea with him. They might be willing to come down in price as they won't have to pay the fees demanded by an auction house. Everything in China is negotiable.

For those who might want a really excellent piece but are unable to afford the prices of a master, you could seek out one of his former apprentices. It is common practice for craftsmen to hone their skills at the feet of a master and take what they have learned and produce very similar pieces at much lower prices.

A good example of this is Yu Ting. Yu Ting has the reputation as the most skilled carver of vases and teapots in China. A tea set carved from the very best dark green jade by his workshop will set you back at least US$100,000. This will be wafer-thin and translucent, with exquisite patterns carved into each piece. They are a joy to behold. There are former apprentices, however, who charge only about US$15,000 for almost the same thing. They will not be quite up to the same standard but are still beautiful.

Then there are humble craftsmen like myself who will charge you less than US$5,000. The advantage of buying a full tea set from me is that mine are practical. You can use them to serve tea. I don't carve them so thin they are fragile to the point that all you can do is admire them. I don't carve exquisite patterns on them. They are made from flawless jade which is made beautifully smooth by intense sanding and polishing. They are a pleasure to handle and a delight to serve tea from and what could be more Chinese than jade and tea served together?

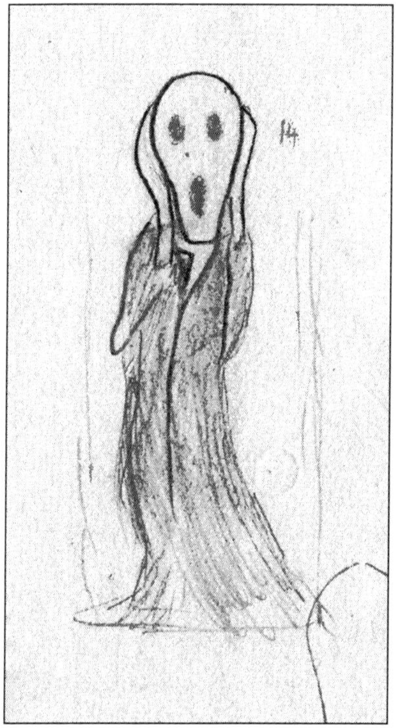

15

The Future

A MODERN JADE workshop would be almost unrecognizable to a craftsman from even the late 1950s. In those distant days, a seasoned carver would either walk or cycle to a state-owned factory. The spindle he used would be operated by treadle. Electricity was available to him, but he would be in his forties or fifties and accustomed to the foot pedals used for generations to drive the simple machinery used to carve stone. He would have little choice in what he carved. This was directed from on high by management. He would work a set number of hours and eat a lunch provided by the factory canteen. At the end of the month he would receive a just a few dollars in pay.

More than thirty years later, in the early 1990s, a successful craftsman would use an electric bike to get to his own workshop. It would already be open and ready for business when he arrived. An apprentice, left to sleep in the workshop overnight to guard the jades, would be at work. The spindle would be electric and the craftsman himself would ink the designs onto the stones to be carved. Lunch would often be cooked in the workshop on a one-ring stove. If a valued customer came to call, they might be treated to a meal at a nearby restaurant.

The profits wouldn't have to be shared with any managers, cleaners, security guards, cooks or administrative staff. When a commission was completed, the master would pick up his mobile phone and let the customer know it was ready. He would come to the workshop and hand over satisfyingly large wads of notes for the finished jade.

Today, less than three decades further on, a successful craftsman might drive to work in a Porsche, BMW or Mercedes. His staff would already be hard at work. Some would be sitting at their desks in front of computer screens using software to design new jades. A technician would be overseeing the computer-driven machines carving the stone. These machines have improved so rapidly over the last decade that they have begun to replace many carvers. Ten years ago, all the machines could do were simple designs. Now they are making three dimensional pieces more efficiently than trained craftsmen.

The machines aren't perfect, however. A technician is in

constant attendance and once a piece has been done, it is given to a craftsman to apply the final touches and make sure there are no problems with it. Their job is no longer the same. They are no longer craftsmen, they are finishers.

Customers rarely come to the workshop. Pieces for sale are viewed online or photos of the jades on offer are sent via one of the modern mobile phone apps like Wechat. The goods are despatched by courier and payment is also received by mobile phone.

These latest changes are the most rapid of all. A few years ago, online payments by mobile phone were unheard of. There were very few couriers taking jades to customers. Computer carving was not good enough for anything but the simplest work. Now in the largest jadeite carving center, Sihui, about half of all small jades are carved in this way.

Every year there are new developments. More and more jades are sold via Taobao, the Chinese equivalent of eBay. And then there is the latest phenomenon, *zhi bo,* mentioned in an earlier chapter, which involves agents who walk around the jade markets and use their mobile phones to broadcast live to thousands of customers at once. It only began in Sihui in the autumn of 2017 but already employs thousands. Daily sales run into millions of dollars.

Online sales are made in different ways in other jade centers. Something similar to *zhi bo* is now catching on in the Temple of the Stone Buddha in Henan. It is concentrated in a very large two-storey building in the center of the wholesale markets. While not exactly the same, it seems to work on the same principle as *zhi bo*. Similar schemes are in operation in carving centers all over China.

A significant number of sales are made using the app Wechat. This is more popular in high-end jade centers such as Suzhou.

For those who are not familiar with it, Wechat is a combination of camera, email, Skype, Facebook and a bank. Jade carvers create their own Wechat groups for their customers and then post photos of what they have for sale. If customers see something they like, they send a private message to the craftsman, agree a price, pay via Wechat and are sent the jade the same day.

There are still plenty of workshops and craftsmen working and selling jade in the traditional way. It is still common for a craftsman to live and work in one small room, but the days of tens of thousands of humble craftsman hunched over their spindles for hours each day crafting individual pieces from start to finish may be numbered. Computers are doing more and more of the work. This won't affect those at the top end of the profession so much. Master carvers will continue to run studios where they take pride in the fact that everything is handmade. Their customers will insist on it.

Another thing that is changing rapidly is health and safety. The lifespans of the previous generation of craftsmen were considerably shortened by inhaling jade particles from the clouds of dust given off by the spindles during carving. Lung problems are common among those who have retired. There are a lot of old carvers who are also deaf or hard of hearing because of the intense noise that carving jade can entail. Many more also suffer from arthritis in their hands and neck as well as spinal problems from being hunched over a spindle clutching a piece of jade for hours on end.

Western jade artists who visit me in China are often horrified at the conditions local carvers work in but the dust masks, extractor fans and ear muffs that have been essential in the West for some time are now beginning to appear in workshops all over China. They are not yet common, but health and safety is something that is being addressed by the two main gem and jewelry associations which oversee the industry. It has been an item at recent board meetings of the largest of these bodies, which has more than half a million members.

This is part of a bigger trend in the more prosperous parts of China. Ordinary people are increasingly concerned about health and safety. When I arrived in Suzhou in 2008, I would never see a person on an e-bike wearing a crash helmet, but it is now quite common. People rarely used the seatbelts in their cars. Now they do. Fewer people are smoking, and more and more people are exercising and going to the gym.

Attitudes are rapidly changing. I used to jog when I first arrived in China. My favorite route was by Jinji Lake. The early morning cleaners and gardeners who tended the gardens used to laugh at me and mimic me running because they thought it was such a strange thing to do. Now, you can't move for joggers, running by the lake every morning. The Suzhou marathon attracts tens of thousands of competitors each year.

But I digress. Back to all things jade. Very few things are certain in this world, but it is clear that Chinese people will always buy jade. It just remains to be seen how long this valuable natural resource lasts. There seems no shortage of lower-quality raw material to satisfy demand for the foreseeable future but it is not so clear where the good material will come from. Each year less and less of the brilliant kingfisher green jadeite from the Kachin Hills in Myanmar and the mutton-fat-white Jade from Hetian in northwest China is found.

There is still plenty of jade around but gem-quality jade is very rare. Finding jade of the right color, translucency and hardness is no easy task. Ask the miners in Canada who export hundreds of tons to China every year. Only the tiniest fraction is top grade.

The best jade is so sought-after that prices are already hundreds of dollars per gram. Walk into one of the many high-end jade shops in Shanghai's famous Yu Yuan tourist district and the sales assistants will tell you with grave faces that there is no more mutton-fat-white jade being mined in China and you must buy now before it's all gone. They have been saying this for years but it could be that in the near future they will at last be telling the truth.

There is so little good material available that many craftsmen can no longer afford to carve it. In Suzhou, famous for small pieces in the best white Hetian jade, more and more Russian white jade is appearing in the shops. Craftsmen wouldn't have looked at this ten years ago. Now they have no choice. It's very good jade and it is a beautiful color, but it is not Hetian jade.

For some time now, they have been using more black jade and what is called porcelain jade. They were low-priced stones ignored by most carvers until a few years ago, but items made with these jades now fetch good prices. Carnelian has also become a popular stone to carve and there are now craftsmen in Suzhou who specialize in it. They have taken to calling it *hong yu* or red jade.

Another recent trend is jade jewelry. Jadeite has been used for jewelry for many years but it's a relatively new thing with nephrite. Look through any book of antique jades and there is very little jewelry. In the twenty-first century, though, it has become commonplace.

One of the reasons is that craftsmen can use a much smaller piece of the best jade and combine it with gold and precious stones to command a high price. Lots of shops now stock jade jewelry and I know of two which sell nothing else.

Some would argue that at the top end of the market, the master carvers and quality craftsmen have nothing to worry about. The masters might not agree. They have seen a dramatic downturn in revenue since the crackdown on corruption by Communist Party chief Xi Jinping who took power in 2012.

High quality jades were a popular gift to give as a bribe to government officials. These officials also loved to buy it for themselves with the "black" money they couldn't deposit in the bank. Now, with more than a million officials being punished for corruption, no one dares give or take a bribe. Or perhaps they are just more discreet. Whichever it is, the master carvers have seen a thirty percent drop in sales.

On the plus side, people are continuing to buy jade. Perhaps fewer people are paying fabulous prices, but one of the effects of the crackdown on corruption is that more money seems to be trickling down to the new middle class in China. They may not have the resources of the corrupt government officials who used to pay tens of thousands of dollars for a jade. But they now seem to have the disposable income to pay several hundred dollars or a few thousand dollars for a piece instead.

When I started to learn to carve in Suzhou's jade alleys, nearly all the customers were wholesalers buying to resell in shops in other cities around China. Now, about half the customers are people looking to buy a piece of jade for themselves or as gift for a friend, family member or loved one. Craftsmen have adapted, prices have tumbled and sales have been good.

Carvers might tell you otherwise, but don't believe them. The clue is in how busy those working in the ancillary services are. The stone cutters, etchers, goldsmiths, polishers and stringers who work with jade have never been busier. When I go to get a piece of stone cut or need to string a finished jade, I have to queue. When I take a jade to the jeweler, they tell me I have to wait at least two weeks or sometimes a month to have it finished. It used to be two or three days.

It is also worth noting that as the amount of high-quality material diminishes year on year, the value of uncut stone and finished pieces will continue to increase. It has become a common practice to invest in very high-quality boulders of uncut jade and leave them in a bank vault to increase in value. There are also plenty of canny carvers with a small stock of the very best stone hidden away.

The masters at the top of the tree may have recently taken a hit in sales but their inventory will only increase in value over time. It is also probably true that multi-millionaire and billionaire collectors and investors will not be put off by astronomically high prices.

I don't believe the current trend of more and more online sales will ever replace the process of a customer going to a gallery. At the top end of the market, the personal touch is ever-more important. Buyers usually love jade as much as the carver, and often long conversations and endless cups of tea are consumed before a purchase is made. The social culture behind such interactions will not disappear so fast.

As China continues to develop, the attitude of people to where the jade for their pendants, bangles and teapots comes from might also change. The conditions for miners in Myanmar are appalling. The jade imported from Yemen is from a conflict zone. The jade from Guatemala is taken out of the country illegally. How long before people in China begin to object to the questionable way their favorite precious stone is acquired?

Customer demand is also changing. The young people of China have very different tastes from their parents. Many of them have traveled extensively and no longer want their jades to be so traditional. While their pockets may not be as deep, they are much more likely to buy more modern and abstract designs. They are more open to new ideas and influences from the West. The new generation of carvers is taking note of what people of their own age want.

This can be seen in *zi gang bei,* one of China's most prestigious annual jade competitions. This is held in Suzhou and attracts exhibits from nearly a thousand of the best carvers from all over China. In 2012, the organizers began to invite Western jade artists to exhibit and compete. While the technical skills of most Western artists fall short of their Chinese counterparts, they tend to be far more creative in their designs.

These outsiders have started to have a profound influence on the work of jade carvers in China. In the last two or three years the jades designed by Chinese craftsmen have begun to show more originality and flair. Gone are the days when every jade at the exhibition would be a traditional design. It is, of course, a two-way process. Western carvers who are invited to exhibit are blown away by the skill levels they see at the exhibition and discover new techniques and tools to improve their craft.

The Suzhou exhibition has become far more prestigious since Western artists began to participate. It now rivals the Beijing competition, *tian gong jiang,* as the main event in China's jade calendar. People are taking note of the work of the new generation of jade artists who feel free to shrug off the shackles of tradition. Their work is already beginning to differ significantly from that of those currently at the top of the profession and this is beginning to show in jade shops around the country.

This doesn't mean traditional design is going to disappear. Jade is part of China's heritage and there are many who buy it because it represents a part of their culture. It is as Chinese as noodles, rice and chopsticks. There isn't a week goes by without a documentary on TV about jade, some Sunday newspapers even have supplements devoted to it, hundreds of books are published every year about it, the museums are full of it and tens of thousands of shops across China sell it.

Jade has been with Chinese people every step of the way

throughout their long history. It is deeply embedded in the national psyche. After all the character for 'country' in the simplified style now used on the mainland (国) is a piece of this precious stone surrounded by four protective walls. But times they are a'changing. It is impossible to predict how people will buy, wear and display this enduring symbol of China in the future, but it will never go away.

In 1990, no one could have foreseen that within twenty years a million people would be working in the jade industry or that the value of the best stone would have increased a thousandfold. In 2010, no one would have predicted that in less than ten years half of all jades would be carved by computer and nearly half of all sales would be conducted and paid for by smartphone. Who knows what the next decades will bring?

Glossary

All Birds Make Obeisance to the Phoenix Hotel: bǎi niǎo cháo fèng jiǔ diàn百鳥朝鳳酒店 Hotel in the area known as The Temple of the Stone Buddha where foreigners are allowed to stay

Anhui: ān huī 安徽 Chinese province notorious for producing high quality copies of ancient jade.

Antique dealer: gǔ wán shāng 古玩商

Antique market: gǔ wán shì chǎng 古玩市場

Antique shop: gǔ wán diàn 古玩店

Badger: gǒu huān 狗獾 Symbolizes happiness. Two badgers double happiness.

Bai Gong Di: bái gōng dì 白工地 Carving district in Bengbu in Anhui province. Noted for its reproductions of jades from previous dynasties and neolithic times.

Bengbu: bèng bù 蚌埠 City in Anhui province with tens of thousands of carvers in five districts who specialize in reproductions of ancient jades.

Can't tell jade from stone: yù shí nán fēn 玉石難分Idiom that means can't tell good from bad.

Carp: lǐ yú 鯉魚. Symbol of the scholar and perseverance.

Chang ming suo: chǎng mìng suǒ 長命鎖. Amulet of protection and long life. Popular gift for children.

Cherchen: qiě mò 且末. Town in Xinjiang province with a market for the jade mined in the Kunlun Mountains.

Chinese moon goddess: cháng é 嫦娥

Empty Tablet: wú zì pái 無字牌A smooth rectangle of unblemished jade which symbolizes a trouble free life. Often worn as a pendant.

Exchange weapons of war for jade and silk: huà gān gē wéi yù bó 化干戈为玉帛. Idiom which means to turn swords into plowshares.

Face: 面子 miàn zǐ. Face in China is a very complicated thing but basically it boils down to the respect which a person can claim from others in their business and social network. People can gain face and lose face by their behavior and the decisions they make.

Fang Gu: fǎng gǔ 仿古. Copies of artifacts from before 1368.

Fei Cui: fěi cuì 翡翠. The name commonly used to describe jadeite.

Flowing Water Jade: shān liú shuǐ 山流水. Jade pebbles and boulders that are found in mountain streams that feed the White and Black Jade Rivers in Hetian in Xinjiang province.

Friends are like gold and jade: yù kūn jīn yǒu 玉昆金友 Chinese idiom which implies friends are extremely precious.

Ghost Market: guǐ shì 鬼市 Legendary market for ancient jade artifacts that operated in Beijing between the hours of midnight and four a.m. in the 1980s and 1990s.

Goldfish: jīn yú 金鱼 Symbolizes a wish for abundance and wealth.

Guan Yu: guān yǔ 关羽 Legendary warrior and general of the Three Kingdoms period. Later worshipped as a God.

Guangfu: guāng fú 光福 Satellite town of Suzhou with its own jade industry specializing in large items mainly using green jade.

Guanxi: guān xì 关系 In the Chinese business world it's the network of relationships among various parties that co-operate and support each other.

Han Dynasty: 206 B.C - 220 A.D. hàn dài 漢代 After the civil war that followed the death of the first emperor, Qin Shihuang, China was reunited under the Han Dynasty.

Have money but no class: yǒu qián méi yǒu wén huà 有钱没有文化 People who flaunt their newly acquired wealth.

Hetian Yu: hé tián yù 和田玉 The name originally used to describe the highly prized nephite jade found in the White and Black Jade rivers in Hetian in northwest China. Now used in China as a classification for all nephrite. If you send a piece of nephrite to one of the official testing centers it doesn't matter where it comes from it will be officially designated as Hetian jade.

Hetian: hé tián 和田 Known in the West as Hotan or Khotan. A town in the Xinjiang region famous for its white jade.

Hongshan civilization: hóng shān wén huà 红山文化 Neolithic culture in an area stretching from Inner Mongolia to Liaoning. 4700 to 2900 BC.

Hostel or guesthouse: bīn guǎn 賓館

Jade and gold on the outside rubbish on the inside: jīn yù qí wài bài xù qí zhōng 金玉其外败絮其中. A Chinese idiom similar to All that glitters is not gold.

Jade bones and ice white skin: yù gǔ bīng jī 玉骨冰肌 Women with slim figures and smooth and fair skin.

Jade Buddha: yù fó 玉佛.

Jade lady: y*ù* nǚ 玉女 A beautiful woman.

Jade Rabbit: yù tù 玉兔 Only companion of the Moon Goddess

Jadeite: fěi cuì 翡翠 Considered one of the two true jades. Jadeite is a mineral from the pyroxene family. It has a hardness on the Mohs Scale of 6.5 - 7 and a specific gravity of 3.25 - 3.4 The chemical formula for jadeite is NaAlSi2O6.

Jieyang: jiē yáng 揭阳. Jadeite carving center in Guangdong province. It specializes in very high quality pieces.

Karakash: Local name for the Black Jade River that flows through Hetian in Xingjiang province. A source of the fabled Hetian seed jade (alluvial pebbles and boulders of nephrite).

Kunlun Mountain Range: kūn lún shān 昆仑山

Lao wai: lǎo wài 老外 The nickname given by people in mainland China to foreigners. It translates as "old outsider." The use of the word "old" in this context is usually a mark of respect.

Liangzhu civilization: liáng zhǔ wén huà 良渚文化 Neolithic culture in the Yangtze River Delta of east China. 3400 - 2250 B.C

Lijiang: 麗江 lì jiāng Jadeite carving center in Yunnan province

Linyi: lín yí 临沂 City in Shandong province

Lion Forest Garden: shī zǐ lín 狮子林 One of Suzhou's famous classical gardens.

Lu Zi Gang: lù zǐ gāng 陆子冈 Ming dynasty craftsman of legendary skill

Magpie: xǐ què 喜鹊 Magical birds seen as messengers of good news and happiness.

Mandarin Ducks: yuān yāng 鸳鸯 Always carved in pairs. A symbol of trust, affection and marital bliss.

Mangshi: máng shì 芒市 Jadeite carving center in Yunnan province.

Ming Dynasty: míng dài 明代 1368 - 1644.

Mountain Jade: shān liào 山料 Jade mined at an alitude of between 2000 and 2500 metres.

Mutton Fat White Jade: yáng zhī bái yù 羊脂白玉 The most valuable white jade in the world. Found in the White Jade River in Hetian.

Myanmar, also known as Burma: miǎn diàn 缅甸 .

Nephrite: ruǎn yù 软玉 Considered one of the two true jades. Nephrite is a variety of the calcium, magnesium, and iron-rich amphibole minerals tremolite or actinolite. It has a hardness on the Mohs Scale of 6 - 6.5 and a specific gravity of 2.9 - 3.01. The chemical formula for nephrite is $Ca_2(Mg, Fe)_5Si_8O_{22}(OH)_2$

New Town Jade Market: xīn cūn yuán liào shì chǎng 新村原料市场 One of the many jade markets at The Temple of the Stone Buddha in Zhengpin in Henan province.

Nüwa: nǚ wā 女娲 The mother goddess of Chinese mythology credited with creating mankind and repairing Heaven.

Oxidized: the surface of the stone which has been modified by oxygen, soil acids etc. In the West this is known as the rind. In China it is called the skin or pi皮.

Pan Jia Yuan: pān jiā yuán. Pan's Family Garden 潘家园. Tourist flea market in Beijing.

Ping An Kou: píng ān kòu 平安扣 Amulet of protection and harmony. Popular gift for children.

Ping An Suo: píng ān suǒ 平安锁 Amulet of protection and a trouble free life. Popular gift for children.

Pingzhou: píng zhōu 平洲 Jadeite carving center in Guangdon province specializing in bangles.

Pi xiu: pí xiū 貔貅 Mythical animal. Symbol for the acquisition and preservation of wealth.

Pure as jade and clean as ice: bīng qīng yù jié 冰清玉洁 A chinese idiom which means to be pure and noble.

Qianlong: 乾隆 qián lóng. Eighteenth century Qing dynasty Emperor. He was a great patron of the arts and loved jade.

Qilin: qí lín 麒麟 Mythical animal sometimes compared to a unicorn. Often placed in the house of a couple who wish for a son. Legend says it will only appear at the time of a good and wise ruler or a great man.

Qimen road: qí mén lù 齐门路 A road where some of the most famous master carvers in China have their workshops.

Qing Dynasty: qīng dài 清代 1644 - 1911.

Qinghai: qīng hǎi 青海 Province just south of the Kunlun mountains with large deposits of white and green nephrite.

Qu Lijun: qú lì jun 瞿利军 Chinese Master Carver who kick started Suzhou's modern jade industry.

Ruan Yu: ruǎn yù 软玉 The term used for nephrite jade.

Ruili: 瑞丽 ruì lì A town in Yunnan province on the border with Myanmar. A Jadeite trading center.

Seed jade: zǐ liào 籽料 Chinese name for the alluvial boulders and pebbles of nephrite found in and around the White and Black Jade rivers in Hetian in Xinjiang province.

Shen Hou: shén hòu 神垕 A wholesale market in Henan for dealers buying and selling copies of jades from the neolithic period to the Qing dynasty.

Shouxing: Chinese god of longevity.

Sihui: sì huì 四会 City in Guangdong province where an estimated 150,000 people work in the jadeite industry. It is the largest jadeite carving center in China and the world.

Silicon carbide: a very hard dark crystalline compound of silicon and carbon that is used as an abrasive

Smooth as jade and soft as flowers: yùruǎn huāróu 玉软花柔 Chinese idiom used to describe a beautiful woman.

Spider: The meaning of a spider carved in jade is Joy from Heaven.

Spindle: A machine used by Chinese craftsmen to carve jade.

Suzhou: sū zhōu 苏州 City in Jiangsu province noted for its small and beautiful carvings in the style of the Ming and Qing dynasties.

Tang Dynasty: táng dài 唐代 618 - 907 Seen as a golden age of culture in Chinese civilization.

Temple of the Stone Buddha: shí fó sì 石佛寺 Largest wholesale nephrite jade market in China. A lot of jadeite is also sold here.

The Chinese Garden of Plentiful Jade: zhōng huá yù bó yuán 中华玉博园. Jade Carving district in Bengbu in Anhui province. Noted for its reproductions of jades from previous dynasties and neolithic times.

The Daylight Market: tiān guāng xū 天光墟 The largest jadeite market in Sihui in Guangdong province. Originally open in the early morning. Now open 24 hours a day.

The Market of Infinite Prosperity: wàn xìng lóng 万兴隆 Jadeite market in Sihui in Guangdong province.

The Resplendent Jade Market. guāng cǎi dà shì chǎng 光彩大市场 One of five districts in Bengbu in Anhui province with hundreds of shops selling copies of jades from previous dynasties.

Tian Gong Jiang: tiān gōng jiāng 天工将 China's most prestigious Jade Carving competition. Roughly translates as The Prize for Heavenly Work. Held each year in Beijing.

To cherish the body as if it was jade: Shǒushēn ruòyù 守身若玉 Chinese idiom which has the western equivalent of "Treat your body like a temple."

Tongcheng: tóng chéng 同城 City in Anhui province with a jade carving district which specializes in high end reproductions of Ming and Qing dynasty jades and copies of work by the legendary Ming dynasty craftsmen Lu Zigang.

Tortoise: wū guī 乌龟 Symbol of longevity.

Uighur: wéi wú ěr zú 维吾尔族 Muslim ethnic minority in Xinjiang province. The main dealers in uncut Hetian jade at markets all over China.

Walking Street: guān qián jiē 观前街 A pedestrian area in the center of old Suzou which has two jade malls and numerous shops selling both jadeite and nephrite.

Warring States period: zhàn guó shí dài戰國時代 475 - 221 B.C.

Weng Zhong: 翁仲 Legendary warrior and bodyguard of the first emperor of China. Worn as an amulet of protection.

Words like gold and jade: jīn yù liáng yán 金玉良言 Invaluable advice.

WuFu: wǔ fú. A jade with five bats carved on it. Signifies the five traditional Chinese blessings of good health, a long life, wealth, love of virtue and a peaceful death in old age.

Xiang Wang Alley: xiàng wáng lòng 相王弄 The main jade carving district in Suzhou.

Xu Shen: xǔ shèn 许慎 Han dynasty scholar and author of the first comprehensive dictionary of Chinese characters.

Xuzhou: xú zhōu 徐州 City in the north of Jiangsu province with a substantial jade carving district.

Yan An Xi qu: yán ān xī qū 延安西区 Jade Carving district in Bengbu in Anhui province. Noted for its reproductions of jades from previous dynasties and neolithic times. Centered on GuangMing Jie.

Yangzhou: yáng zhōu 扬州 City in Jiangsu province with a tradition of carving large jade sculptures, especially mountain scenes. The home of the last remaining government jade factory.

Ying Yu: yìng yù 硬玉 A name used to describe Jadeite. Translates as "Hard Jade."

Yingjiang: yíng jiāng 盈江 A town in Yunnan province which specializes in the sale of rough uncut jadeite boulders.

You get what you pay for: yī fèn jià qián yī fèn huò
一分价钱一分货

Yurungkash: Local name for the White Jade River in Hetian in Xinjiang province north west China.

Zhi Bo: zhí bō 直播 Online trading platforms in China

Bibliography

CHEN SHEN and Gu Fang, *Ancient Chinese Jades from the Royal Ontario Museum,* 2013, Cultural Relics Press.

Hughes, Richard W. Galibert, Olivier. Bosshart, George. Ward, Fred. Oo Thet. Smith, Mark. Tay Thye Sun & Harlow George. *Burmese Jade: The Inscrutable Gem* http://www.ruby-sapphire.com/jade_burma_part_1.htm

Yu Weili, *Chinese Jade Carving - Famous Beijing Carvers and their work*, 2008, SJCP Press. 中国玉雕-北京名家名品 编著-俞伟理

Yu Weili, *Chinese Jade Carving - Famous Nanyang Carvers and their work*, 2008, SJCP Press. 中国玉雕-南阳名家名品 编著-俞伟理

Yu Weili, *Chinese Jade Carving - Famous Yangzhou Carvers and their work*, 2008, SJCP Press. 中国玉雕-扬州名家名品 编著-俞伟理

He Wan and Cai Ying, *Chinese Jade Carving Master -Qu Li Jun,* 2012, 中国玉石雕刻大师 - 瞿利军

Ao Yan, *Chinese Jade Carving Master Yangxi*, 2009, Geology Press 地址出版社 南石东曦 - 中国玉石雕刻大师 - 杨曦

Gu Fang and Li Hongjuan, *Chinese Jade. The Spiritual and Cultural Signifance of Jade in China,* 2013, Shanghai Press

BIBLIOGRAPHY

Williams, C.A.S, *Chinese Symbolism and Art Motifs*, 1974, Tuttle Publishing.

Shan Cunde, 單存德 *A History of Carving and Engraving (in Suzhou) Diaolouningxhang*, 2015, Fenghuang Press 鳳凰出版社

Gemological Institute of America, *Gem Reference Guide*, 1988, GIA Press

Huo Da, The Jade King, 1992, Panda Press

Suzhou's Contemporary Master Carvers (苏州手工艺当代人物志 - 翠玉珠宝), 2018, Guwuxuan Press (古吴轩出版社)

Mr. Warry of the Chinese Consular Service, *Hertz's Burma Gazetteer: Myitkyina District (1912)* Virtually the only account in English of the early history of jadeite in then-Burma.

Ward, Fred and Charlotte, Jade, 2015, Gem Books.

Goette, John, *Jade Lore*, 1936, Kelly and Walsh.

Gump, Richard, *Jade: Stone of Heaven, 1962,* **Doubleday**

Forsyth, Angus and McElney, Brian, *Jades from China,* 1994, The Museum of East Asian Art.

Beck, Russell and Mason, Maika, *Pounamu,* 2010, Penguin

Chen Hailu, Selected works of the Suzhou Jade Carver Jiangxi, 2008, China Academy of Arts Press

Fang Jingpei, *Symbols and Rebuses in Chinese Art*, 2004, Ten Speed Press;

Levy, Adrian and Scott-Clark, Cathy, *The Stone of Heaven. The Secret History of Imperial Green Jade,* 2002, Weidenfield and Nicolson.

Haiyan Lee, *The Stranger and the Chinese Moral Imagination*, 2018, Stanford University Press.

Barnes, Gina L, *Understanding Chinese Jade in a world context,* 2018, Journal of the British Academy 6: 1- 63

Zacke, Irene M, *Auction Catalog of Archaic and Antique Chinese Jades*, 2018, Galerie Zacker.

Cheng Menghui, *A Dictionary of Commonly Used Chinese idioms,* 2006, Commercial Press International.

Friends of Jade. Originally a newsletter which originated in the UK in the 1980s for people with a love of jade. It metamorphosed into a website in the 1990s which has a lot of useful information on jade. It can also be found as a closed group on Facebook.

Xin Hong, Chinese Art Auction Records - Jade, 2010, Hunan Fine Arts

Xin Hong, Chinese Art Auction Records - Jade, 2018, Hunan Fine Arts

Acknowledgments

I WOULD LIKE to give special thanks to Chris Jiang in Beijing, Qu Lijun in Suzhou and Zhang Jinhong in Sihui without whose help I would not have been able to write this book. They are also listed among the following people who were very generous with their time and knowledge. My gratitude goes to them all.

Angus Forsyth: Jade collector and author. Hong Kong.

Ao Yan: (奥岩) Chairman of the Beijing BoGuan International Auction House.

Cheng Huo: (程浩) General manager of Yangzhou Arts and Crafts Group.

Chenglong Jiang (蒋成龙): Assistant Director of the Academic Research Division of China's Collectors Association.

Dave Dunford.

Gu Fang: (古方) Executive Director of the Institute of Traditional Culture and Social Responsibility of Beijing University. Author of books on jade and renowned Jade Scholar.

Huang Hezhong: Jade expert and writer. Suzhou.

Kirk Makepeace: Jade West. Canada.

Li Hanzhou: Director of the Sihui Jade and Jewellery Industry Development Centre.

Mary Lou Ridinger: Jade Maya. Guatemala.

Qu Lijun: (瞿利军) Chinese Jade Carving Master, Suzhou.

Wufan (吴凡) Jade Craftsman, Suzhou.

Zhang Jinhong: (張锦洪). Owner of 汇玉堂 and the World Museum of Jade in Sihui, Guangdong.

Yao Shuming (姚树明) in Bengbu

Yang Shixin (杨仕信) Jade Craftsman. Suzhou.

Zhen Qing (郑青). Gem and Jewelry Trade Association of China GAC. Jade Department.

John Westbrooke

About The Author

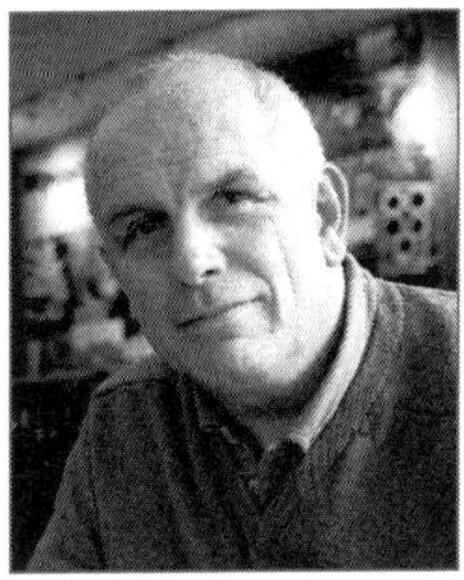

Andrew Shaw grew up in north London and worked as a senior reporter for the BBC General News Service before moving to China to learn the art of jade carving in 2008. In a few short years, he became a gold medal-winning master carver. He lives with his wife in the city of Suzhou near Shanghai where he has a studio and gallery. *www.jadefiend.com*